Damascus

Jessica Lee

Credits

Footprint credits
Editor: Alan Murphy
Production and Layout: Patrick Dawson,
Elysia Alim, Danielle Bricker
Maps: Kevin Feeney

Managing Director: Andy Riddle
Commercial Director: Patrick Dawson
Publisher: Alan Murphy
Publishing Managers: Felicity Laughton,
Nicola Gibbs
Digital Editors: Jo Williams, Tom Mellors
Marketing and PR: Liz Harper
Sales: Diane McEntee
Advertising: Renu Sibal
Finance and Administration: Elizabeth
Taylor

Photography credits
Front cover: Thiele Klaus/4 corners
Back cover: RCH/Shutterstock

Printed in Great Britain by CPI Antony Rowe,
Chippenham, Wiltshire

Every effort has been made to ensure that
the facts in this guidebook are accurate.
However, travellers should still obtain
advice from consulates, airlines, etc about
travel and visa requirements before travelling.
The authors and publishers cannot accept
responsibility for any loss, injury or
inconvenience however caused.

Publishing information
Footprint *Focus Damascus*
1st edition
© Footprint Handbooks Ltd
July 2011

ISBN: 978 1 908206 04 6
CIP DATA: A catalogue record for this book
is available from the British Library

® Footprint Handbooks and the Footprint
mark are a registered trademark of Footprint
Handbooks Ltd

Published by Footprint
6 Riverside Court
Lower Bristol Road
Bath BA2 3DZ, UK
T +44 (0)1225 469141
F +44 (0)1225 469461
www.footprintbooks.com

Distributed in the USA by Globe Pequot Press,
Guilford, Connecticut

The content of Footprint *Focus Damascus* has
been taken directly from Footprint's *Syria
Handbook*, which was researched and written
by Jessica Lee.

Contents

Ancient and beautiful, Damascus doesn't fail to enchant. The Old City is a maze of creaky old buildings that slump over twisting, narrow alleyways and getting lost is a mandatory part of the experience. During the day the winding streets of this fascinating quarter are alive with the bustle of shoppers and sightseers bargaining over goods in the souqs, while in the evening, old men dust off their backgammon boards and set up camp outside on the pavement, engrossed in battle.

At the heart of it all is the Umayyad Mosque, its huge dome and minarets rising majestically above its surroundings. But the mosque's history, just like that of the city itself, stretches back far beyond Islamic times. This is the city where St Paul was baptized and began his preaching, where all the great trade routes of the world once converged in an ancient hub of commerce. Local legend even claims that this is the setting of the original Garden of Eden. It's no wonder that Damascus lays claim to the title of oldest continuously inhabited city in the world.

Look a little deeper behind this picturesque daydream of a city and you'll notice the vibrant modern progress as well. Tourism is booming here and behind nondescript doors in dusty alleys lie sumptuous palaces restored to their former glory as boutique hotels and restaurants. If you want to live out any Arabian Nights- style fairytale then this is the place to splash out and do it. Young, upwardly mobile Syrians flock to the pavement-terraces of European-style cafés that have brought cappuccino culture to the city. Outside the walls the sprawling metropolis of the new town may not be as pretty as the Old City but is host to the fabulous National Museum, a must-see for anyone interested in Syria's history.

If you can pull yourself away from exploring the Old City's nooks and crannies, there are several day trips that can be comfortably made from here, including the cliff-side village of Maaloula, where they still speak the language of Christ and the black basalt ruins of Bosra to the south, one of Syria's best preserved Roman era sights.

Planning your trip

Best time to visit

Syria is at its best during spring (late March to early June) and autumn (early September to early November). During both these seasons temperatures are pleasantly mild (15-20°C). Spring is when the country is at its greenest, the wild flowers are in full blossom and the showers and cooler air mean that the atmosphere is free from haze, so you get the best views. During the summer (early June to early September) it is generally very hot and dry, with temperatures averaging 30°C and sometimes reaching above 40°C, particularly from mid-July to mid-August. Sightseeing in such conditions can be very hard work. Winter (mid-November to mid-March) by contrast can be bitterly cold, temperatures often fall close to freezing and this is also when the majority of the rainfall comes.

Another element to factor into planning, is *Ramadan* (the Muslim month of fasting). During this month Muslims do not drink, eat or smoke from sunrise to sunset and although non-Muslims are not expected to join in, you should refrain from eating, drinking and smoking in public. Also, many smaller businesses will close during daylight hours and some will not open for the entire month, although shops and tourist sites are open as normal. Travelling in Syria at this time can be frustrating but if you do find yourself here during *Ramadan* you will probably be rewarded by constant invitations to share *Iftar* (the evening meal that breaks the daily fast) with the many Syrians that you meet, leaving you with an unforgettable insight into Islam and Arab culture. For the dates of *Ramadan*, see page 14.

Getting there

Air

Syria's two international airports are in Damascus and Aleppo. Damascus is the main hub with more connections to Europe (see page 20). Both airports have flights to other Middle Eastern destinations. Direct flights to Syria are accessible and affordable from Europe but for cheap flights from Australasia and North America you will need to shop around a bit. Flights from both destinations will involve at least one stopover en route. For the cheapest possible flights, consider flying to another Middle Eastern country and travelling overland, or booking an onward flight, from there. Recommended online booking agencies where you can compare airfares include www.expedia.com, www.cheapflights.com and www.skyscanner.net.

Flights from UK The cheapest direct flights from London start at UK£300 with **BMI** (www.flybmi.com), who have daily flights to Damascus. **British Airways** (www.britishairways.com) and **Syrian Air** (www.syriaair.com) both also fly direct. Cheaper deals are available if you don't mind a lengthy stopover on the way. Good options include **Austrian Airlines** (www.aua.com), **Royal Jordanian** (www.rj.com), **Emirates** (www.emirates.com) and **Turkish Airlines** (www.thy.com).

An even cheaper option would be to fly from London to Istanbul and then travel overland to the border. Both **Easyjet** (www.easyjet.com) and **Pegasus Airlines** (www.pegasusairlines.com) have flights from London to Istanbul for as little as UK£39.

Flights from the rest of Europe Syrian Air (www.syriaair.com) has direct flights from several European cities. Other airlines that provide direct flights include **Air France** (www.airfrance.com), **Austrian Airlines** (www.aua.com), **Alitalia** (www.alitalia.com), **Cyprus Airways** (cyprusairways.com) and **Czech Airlines** (czechairlines.com). Flights start from an average of EU£400.

Flights from North America There are no direct flights to Syria from North America. To get the best deal you can either fly to London or another European city first, or via another city in the Middle East. Both **Emirates** (www.emirates.com), and **Etihad** (www.etihadairways.com), fly via the Gulf States and onward to Damascus. Flights to Damascus, via Dubai, from Los Angeles and New York start from US$700 one way or US$1100 return.

Flights from Australia and New Zealand Flights from Australia via Dubai cost from AU$1400 one-way or AU$1800 return. It is usually cheaper looking into flights to other Middle Eastern destinations such as Istanbul, Dubai and Amman and booking separate onward flights or overland travel to Syria from there. It's worth noting that from Dubai the new airline **Flydubai** (www.flydubai.com) offers daily flights to Damascus and Aleppo from US$80.

For airport departure tax information, see page 15.

Getting around

Travel between the main centres in Syria is relatively easy and cheap. The bus network stretches nearly all over the country while the recently improved rail network is a good option in the west. If you are travelling by public transport, some of the more far-flung sights (particularly the **Dead Cities** and the **Euphrates** region) provide more of a challenge to visit. It's worthwhile hiring a car/driver to save time, but with careful planning, and a lot of patience, it's not impossible to visit most sights using a combination of public transport and negotiating rides with locals.

Air As Syria is small enough to travel around by road, domestic flights are pretty unnecessary. For those with very limited time, **Syrian Air** (www.syriaair.com) operate reasonably priced flights from **Damascus** to **Aleppo**, **Lattakia**, **Deir ez-Zor** and **Qamishle** (see page 59).

Road
Bus There are plenty of privately owned bus companies operating large air-conditioned coach services (known as **Pullman** buses) between the main centres in Syria. Due to competition prices tend to be cheap and services frequent and, in general, you don't have to pre-book tickets. Of the many companies, **Kadmous** and **Al-Ahliah** seem to operate the most extensive routes. All Pullman bus services are non-smoking except for the driver, so if you have problems with cigarette fumes be sure to ask for a seat towards the back of the bus. On many routes you will need to show your passport to purchase tickets.

As well as the Pullmans there are still some old mid-size buses (known as **Hob-hob** buses) plying routes between the smaller towns. Services tend to leave when the bus is full and are generally cheaper (and slower) then the Pullman buses.

Microbus Although cramped, uncomfortable and hot (in summer), **microbuses** provide transport to many of the smaller places that the big Pullman buses don't service. They are particularly useful for routes between smaller towns along the coast and the Orontes Valley, and getting to sights such as Apamea, The Dead Cities and Krak des Chevaliers. Microbuses leave from their own garages (usually a dusty parking lot) and there are no set departure times so you just need to turn up, ask around and wait for the next service to leave (usually when it's full).

Car Hiring a car is an attractive option in Syria, particularly if you intend to visit remoter areas where public transport can be erratic or non-existent. The vast majority of car-hire firms are based in Damascus, though centres like Aleppo and Lattakia also have branches of the international car-hire firms. While the local companies are sometimes significantly cheaper than the international ones (some offer cars for as little as US$30 per day, as opposed to an average of around US$60 per day), it is very important to check the rental conditions and insurance cover carefully, as some smaller local companies don't offer any cover other than third party with their vehicles. In such cases, if you have an accident you will usually be liable for the full cost of the repairs. If you have an accident, make sure you obtain a police report; without one, even full insurance arrangements may be invalidated.

The minimum age for car hire varies between 21 and 25. Most companies require that you have held a full licence for at least one year. An international driving licence is not compulsory, although it is useful to have one in any case. Most companies have a minimum rental period of three days. There is usually a choice between limited mileage (usually up to 125 km) and unlimited mileage; unless you are sure that you are not going to be covering any great distances, it generally works out cheaper in the end to go for unlimited mileage. Most companies require either a credit card or a cash deposit, usually in the region of US$500-1000.

Budget (www.budget-sy.com) and **Europcar** (www.europcar-middleeast.com) are two of the main international car-rental firms in Syria. Both have offices in Damascus and Aleppo. With **Budget**, the minimum rental period is three days, with small car rental starting from US$55 per day with unlimited mileage. A medium-sized car starts from US$75. You have to pay a deposit (credit cards accepted) of US$600, which you get back when you return the car. Europcar's rates tend to be higher: with limited mileage and a three-day rental, small cars start from US$80 per day and medium-sized cars from US$90 per day, but if you are renting a car for more than one week the daily rate drops substantially. **Marmou Car Hire** (www.marmou.com) is a good local car-hire company with offices in Damascus. Their rates are as low as US$35 per day for the cheapest car, with their most expensive car US$80 per day. They have excellent weekly rental rates from US$220-500. Car hire has limited mileage of 120 km per day with an extra charge of 30 cents per kilometre if you go over this. All car rentals include full insurance.

Train

The Syrian train network has vastly improved in recent years making train travel a viable and inexpensive option for travellers, at least along the main route between Damascus and Aleppo and to the coast, from Aleppo to Lattakia. Both routes boast comfortable new air-conditioned trains.

First-class tickets are good value and are worthwhile. There are five services per day between Damascus and Aleppo but be aware that some departures are in the very early morning hours, or in the evening, denying passengers of any views en route. The journey between Aleppo and Lattakia is particularly beautiful. Always take your passport when buying train tickets.

For most of the rest of the country train travel is unfeasible due to lacklustre services, inconvenient departure times, old and uncomfortable carriages and inconveniently placed railway stations that are far out of towns.

Sleeping

Most of the main cities and tourism centres have a reasonable amount of accommodation for all budgets. Many smaller towns tend to have one or two hotels, usually in the mid-range or budget categories. In Damascus and Aleppo, a burgeoning number of old Ottoman houses and palaces have recently been converted into atmospheric and unusual top-end hotels, making a welcome addition to the luxury market, which had until now been dominated by the chain-hotels.

Be aware that hotel facilities, even in the top-end bracket, are usually not to the same standard as the West. Hot water can be erratic in all but the luxury end of the market. Many mid-range hotel rooms may boast TV and air-conditioning but that doesn't mean they work. It is always wise to ask to see the room and check that everything works before actually checking in. Making up for a shortfall with facilities, hotel staff are usually incredibly helpful and eager to please.

While the lower mid-range and budget hotels accept payment in S£s, practically all hotels from **$$$** category upwards prefer to be paid in US$. Just to confuse things, many mid-range and top-end hotels in Aleppo prefer to be paid in Euro. Most luxury and mid-range hotels now also accept major credit cards. Nearly all hotels above **$$** category also charge an extra 10% government tax; be sure to check whether this is included in the price you are quoted. See box, on next page , for details of hotel price categories.

Hotels in some places, most notably Palmyra and to a lesser extent Hama, show marked variations in prices between the low and high seasons. In the case of Palmyra, the high season is March-April and August-December, while in Hama it is April-May and July-October. Elsewhere, prices generally stay stable throughout the year, although there are small variations in some categories in Damascus, where the high season is during the summer months (July-October).

Camping

There are very few official campsites in Syria. Beside the Damascus–Aleppo motorway just outside Damascus, the government-run **Harasta** campsite is a thoroughly unappealing place: noisy, with little natural shade and very basic toilet/shower facilities. By contrast, the privately run **Camping Kaddour** to the west of Aleppo is very pleasant and Palmyra has a lovely campground amidst the date palms.

Providing you have your own equipment, there are plenty of opportunities for 'unofficial' camping. The coastal Jebel Ansariye mountains are probably the most beautiful area, with plenty of attractive woodlands complete with streams and waterfalls offering idyllic sites. Camping at some of the more remote historic monuments and

Sleeping and eating price codes

Sleeping

$$$$ over US$150		**$$$**	US$66-150
$$ US$30-65		**$**	Under US$30

Price codes refer to the cost of two people sharing a double room in the high season.

Eating

¶¶¶	Expensive over US$12	¶¶	Mid-range US$6-12
¶	Cheap under US$6		

Prices refer to the average cost of a two-course meal for one person, not including drinks or service charge.

---

archaeological sites is also an option, although you should ask permission first. In more populated areas, camping will certainly generate a great deal of curiosity amongst local people, and in all likelihood you will be invited to stay in someone's house; trying to persuade them that you actually want to camp may be difficult.

Eating and drinking → For Arabic cuisine, see page 79.

Food

Syria's cuisine is essentially classic Arabic fare. **Meat**, in the form of lamb or chicken, features fairly prominently in the Arab diet, along with staples such as chickpeas (in the form of falafels or hummus), rice, salads and mezze, and of course bread (*khubz*). Despite the prominence of meat in the diet, **vegetarians** can be sure of a nutritious and reasonably varied diet with the wide variety of predominantly vegetable-based mezze dishes on offer.

When Syrian food is done well, it is delicious, and in Damascus and Aleppo there are a host of excellent restaurants where the menu selections are varied and imaginative. Be aware that in many smaller towns though, you will find yourself confronted with a rather predictable choice of roast chicken, meat kebabs, hummus, salad and chips. Those on a tight budget will find the choice particularly monotonous with a diet made up of *shawarma* and falafel and the occasional half roast chicken.

International cuisine and **fast food** are available in the bigger towns and in the restaurants of the luxury hotels.

Drink

Tea and **coffee** compete as the national drinks. Both are served in the usual Arabic way and if you ask for milk it will be usually powdered or UHT. If you prefer instant coffee you need to ask for *Nescafe*. You can get excellent freshly squeezed **fruit juices** all over the country, and **fizzy drinks** and **mineral water** are widely available.

Although bars are not that common outside of Damascus, many visitors are surprised at how readily available **alcohol** is in what is a predominantly Muslim country. This reflects the diverse nature of society in Syria (Christians account for around 10% of the population), and also its essentially tolerant nature. Wine, locally brewed and imported beers and *arak* (the Arabic liqueur) are available at many restaurants and liquer stores, while imported spirits are usually obtainable from the more top-end eateries and hotels.

Locally brewed beers include *Al-Chark*, from Aleppo and *Barada* from Damascus. Neither are particularly good and you have to watch out for out-of-date bottles, but when fresh and properly chilled, they are certainly drinkable. Look out for the excellent imported Lebanese lagers *Al-Maaza* and *Lazziza*, which are both excellent.

Responsible tourism

Clothing Syrians place a lot of importance on smartness and cleanliness and making the effort to be presentable in public will earn you greater respect. Singlets, low-cut tops, bare midriffs, above-the-knee shorts and skirts and other skimpy clothing are not acceptable dress in Syria and often cause offence. The key to remember is shoulders and knees (and everything in-between) should be covered at all times. This rule applies to men as well as women. See also 'Visiting mosques' below.

Conduct Syrians are incredibly welcoming and open and will go out of their way to help foreigners. Return this gesture by being equally polite and friendly.

Making the effort to use a little of the language will be greatly appreciated. Syrians are always ecstatically happy and surprised when a foreigner speaks Arabic, even if it is only a few words. Except among more cosmopolitan people it is not usual for a man and a woman to shake hands when meeting. Instead place your right hand across your heart; this can also be used as a sign of thank you as well. Open displays of affection between couples are not acceptable in public and can cause great offence. Conversely, it is completely normal for friends of the same sex (male and female) to hold hands and link arms in public.

While eating a shared meal like mezze, it's acceptable to use your left hand to tear bread but the right hand should be used to take from the communal bowls and also to pass things to people. Always tuck your feet in towards you when sitting down. Feet are considered unclean and it's very rude to point them at someone. Also, crossing your legs while seated is considered rude by some more conservative people.

Visiting mosques Non-Muslims are welcome in most mosques in Syria, although in some Shi'ite mosques they are only allowed into the courtyard and not the prayer hall itself. In any case, always seek permission before entering a mosque. Remember that shoes must be removed before entering the prayer hall, although socks can be left on. It is very important that both men and women dress modestly, covering arms and legs (shorts are not acceptable) and in the case of women, wearing a headscarf. At larger, more important mosques, such as the Umayyad Mosque in Damascus, women are required to hire a full-length black hooded robe at the entrance (and men also if they attempt to enter in shorts).

Essentials A-Z

Accident and emergency
In the event of an emergency contact the relevant service: (police T112, ambulance T110, traffic police T115, fire T113), and your embassy (see below). An official police/medical report is required for insurance claims.

Electricity
220 volts, 50 AC. European 2-pin sockets are the norm. Electricity supply is on the whole reliable, although power cuts do occur (particularly in Aleppo).

Festivals and events
For further details on festivals contact the Ministry of Tourism (www.syriatourism.org).

April/May
Palmyra Desert Festival This major event runs for 3 days and draws locals as well as foreign visitors. In the day there is a full programme of horse and camel racing, while the evenings host performances of folk dancing and traditional music in the restored Roman theatre in the midst of the ruins.

July/August
Jazz Lives In Syria Festival This annual festival brings international artists to Damascus and Aleppo for 1 week of concerts. For more information visit www.jazzlivesinsyria.com.

September
Bosra Festival This festival uses Bosra's huge Roman theatre as a venue for a lively programme of music, singing, dancing and drama, with many visiting acts from abroad. The festival dates change yearly, for further details visit www.bosrafestival.org.
Silk Road Festival Organized by the Ministry of Tourism, this annual event stages cultural performances celebrating the history of the trade routes. Concerts and events are held in Damascus, Aleppo and Palmyra.

Public holidays
The following dates are fixed public holidays; many of the major Muslim and Christian holidays are also public holidays, although their dates vary from year to year. Only those holidays marked * are celebrated nationally; the remainder are celebrated in a limited way, perhaps with a cultural event and certain government offices closing, or in the case of something like Marine's Day, with that section of the armed forces having a holiday.

1 Jan New Year's Day*
22 Feb Union Day
8 Mar Revolution Day*
22 Mar Arab League Day
17 Apr Independence Day*
1 May Workers' Day*
6 May Martyrs' Day*
29 May Marine's Day
6 Oct Veteran's Day
16 Oct Flight Day
16 Nov Correctionist Movement Day
14 Dec Peasants' Day
25 Dec Christmas Day*

Islamic holidays
Islamic holidays are calculated according to the lunar calendar and therefore fall on different dates each year (see box, page 14), for projected dates from 2010-2013).

Health
See your GP or travel clinic at least 6 weeks before departure for general advice on travel risks and vaccinations. Try phoning a specialist travel clinic if your own doctor is unfamiliar with health conditions in Syria. Make sure you have sufficient medical travel insurance, get a dental check, know your

own blood group and if you suffer a long-term condition such as diabetes or epilepsy, obtain a Medic Alert bracelet/necklace (www.medicalert.co.uk). If you wear glasses, take a copy of your prescription.

Vaccinations

It is advisable to vaccinate against **polio**, **diphtheria**, **tetanus**, **typhoid**, **hepatitis A** and **hepatitis B**. If you're going to more remote areas consider having the **rabies** vaccination. You are not required to show a yellow-fever vaccination certificate on arrival unless you are arriving from a yellow-fever-infected country. You may also be required to show a vaccination certificate if you have visited a yellow-fever-infected country at any stage during the last month and may be turned away if you can't produce one. The occurrence of malaria is rare in Syria though there have been reported cases. It is sensible to avoid being bitten as much as possible; cover bare skin and use an insect repellent. The most common and effective repellent is diethyl metatoluamide (DEET). DEET liquid is best for arms and face (take care around eyes and with spectacles; DEET dissolves plastic). Aerosol spray is good for clothes and ankles and liquid DEET can be dissolved in water and used to impregnate cotton clothes and mosquito nets. Impregnated wrist and ankle bands can also be useful. Contact your travel clinic before travel to find out up-to-date information on malaria-risk and discuss anti-malarial drugs.

Health risks

Stomach upsets are common among travellers to Syria. They're mainly caused by the change in diet (Syrian food is heavy on oil which can be hard to digest for people unused to this diet). The most common cause of prolonged travellers' **diarrhoea** is from eating contaminated food or drinking tap water. Diarrhoea may be also caused by viruses, bacteria (such as E-coli), protozoal

(such as giardia), salmonella and cholera. It may be accompanied by vomiting or by severe abdominal pain. Any kind of diarrhoea responds well to the replacement of water and salts. Sachets of rehydration salts can be bought in most chemists and can be dissolved in water. If the symptoms persist, consult a doctor. To avoid diarrhoea, drink only bottled or boiled water, avoid having ice in drinks and peel fruit and vegetables before eating. Use your sense when choosing a restaurant; if it's a busy, popular place it's more likely to be safe to eat there and food is more likely to be fresh.

In the summer months **heat exhaustion** and **heatstroke** are common health risks in Syria. This is prevented by drinking enough fluids throughout the day (your urine will be pale if you are drinking enough). Symptoms of heat exhaustion and heatstroke are similar and include dizziness, tiredness and headache. Use lots of fluids or better, rehydration salts mixed with water, to replenish fluids and salts and find somewhere cool and shady to recover.

If you suspect heatstroke rather than heat exhaustion, you need to cool the body down quickly (cold showers are particularly effective) and may require hospital treatment for electrolyte replacement by intravenous drip.

Money
Currency

→ €1=S£68; £1=S£78; US$1=S£47 *(May 2011)*
The basic unit of currency is the Syrian pound (S£) or lira. Notes come in denominations of S£1000, S£500, S£100 and S£50. Coins come in denominations of S£25, S£10, S£5, S£2 and S£1. The division of the S£ into 100 piastres is largely redundant.

Changing money

The influx of **ATM** machines over the past few years has made travelling in Syria much easier. The **Commercial Bank of Syria (CBS)** has ATMs in most medium-sized towns but their machines sometimes don't accept foreign cards (even if they display Maestro, Visa and Cirrus network signs). Cards linked to the maestro network tend to have the most problems. ATMs linked to branches of the **Bank of Syria and Overseas** are usually reliable for most foreign debit/credit cards. Damascus, Aleppo, Hama, Homs, Lattakia and Tartus all have reliable ATMs but in smaller towns you may run into problems and it is not sensible to depend solely on using ATMs.

It's still advisable to carry plenty of **cash** (in US$) for the times when an ATM won't accept your card and for the smaller towns. Cash can be changed at most banks (including branches of CBS), and exchange offices (which are open for longer hours than the banks). Most mid and top-range hotels also prefer to be paid in US$.

These days **traveller's cheques (TCs)** are more a hindrance than a help in Syria and you'd be better off using a mixture of ATM withdrawals and cash. Changing TCs is a lengthy and involved process that can take up an entire morning. Branches of **CBS** change TCs and charge a flat fee of S£25 per transaction.

Most major **credit cards** (Visa, MasterCard, American Express, Diners Club) are accepted at the more expensive hotels and restaurants, and at larger tourist souvenir and handicraft shops in the main cities. They can also be used to pay for airline tickets and car hire. Note that over-the-counter bank cash advances are officially not possible in Syria. That said, the situation is becoming much more relaxed and some of the luxury hotels, large shops and several private companies are willing to do so. If you need a cash advance ask at your hotel or anywhere displaying a Visa, MasterCard or American Express sign. Be aware that you will have to pay a hefty fee for the service.

Using the **black market** won't save you any money as the rates offered are the same as the banks. The black market is most active in the area around Martyrs Sq in Damascus and in the city souqs. If you need to change money outside of banking hours ask at your hotel reception. Staff are usually happy to exchange cash at the official bank rate.

Changing S£ back into hard currency is very difficult in Syria. If you are flying out, be aware that the airport bank won't change S£ into dollars either. It's really a case of trying not to end up with too many S£s left over. If you are leaving overland there is no problem in changing S£ at the Jordanian, Lebanese and Turkish border.

Cost of living and travelling

The cost of living and travelling in Syria is far cheaper than in Europe or North America and in comparison to neighbouring Lebanon, Jordan and Turkey, travel in Syria can be very economical. Be aware though that prices have risen dramatically over the past couple of years and how much you spend will depend not only on the degree of comfort you want to travel in, but also on how much you want to do in a given amount of time.

Accommodation will be your biggest expense in Syria, especially in Damascus and Aleppo where rooms are in high demand. In contrast, eating out is remarkably cheap, even in the fanciest restaurants. A 2-course meal in an expensive restaurant rarely works out at more than US$10-15 per head and those on tight budgets will rarely pay over US$2 per meal by existing on a diet of mostly *shawarma* and *falafel*.

Travelling by public transport is inexpensive with tickets seldom costing over US$4. If you plan on hiring a car/driver budget approximately US$60-100 per day for travel costs. Entry fees to major museums and sites are cheap but if you plan on seeing a lot they can add up. Entry costs S£75 for small sites and S£150 for larger ones but

Islamic holidays (approximate dates)

Holiday	2010	2011	2012	2013
Islamic New Year	18 Dec 2009 (1431)	9 Dec 2010 (1432)	26 Nov 2011 (1433)	15 Nov 2012 (1434)
Moulid an-Nabi (Prophet's birthday)	26 Feb	15 Feb	4 Feb	24 Jan
Leilat al-Meiraj	8 Jul	28 Jun	16 Jun	5 Jun
Ramadan	11 Aug	1 Aug	20 Jul	9 Jul
Eid al-Fitr	10 Sep	30 Aug	19 Aug	8 Aug
Eid al-Adha	16 Nov	6 Nov	26 Oct	15 Oct

those with an international student card (ISIC) are given huge discounts.

Those on tight budgets can exist on about US$25 per day by living on a diet of *shawarma* and *falafel* and by staying in the cheapest of budget hotels and using dormitories where available. A budget of US$50-70 per day would be much more comfortable and would allow you to eat a more varied diet, stay in decent budget/mid-range accommodation and hire a car/driver for the more out-of-the-way sights. Luxury travel (boutique hotels, the best restaurants and a private vehicle, perhaps with driver and guide), means moving into the equivalent price ranges as for luxury travel in Europe and North America; basically from US$150-200 per day upwards.

Opening hours

Banks, post offices and government offices are usually open Sat-Thu 0800-1400, though in the cities some banks and post offices open until 1700. Official shop opening hours are Sat-Thu 0800-1400 and 1600-1800, but many now open throughout the day especially in the larger towns. Museums and sights are normally open from 0900-1800 in summer (Apr-Sep) and from 0900-1600 in winter (Oct-Mar). Most close on Tue though there are exceptions to the rule.

Prohibitions

If you do find yourself in legal trouble in Syria be aware that your embassy cannot help you get out of trouble, but they are a useful source of advice for seeking translators and English-speaking lawyers. For a list of embassies in Damascus, see page 61.

Drugs

Possession of narcotics is illegal in Syria. Those caught in possession risk a long prison sentence and/or deportation. There is a marked intolerance to drug-taking in Syria and the drugs scene is distinctly seedy (not to mention paranoid) and best avoided.

Photography

Avoid taking pictures of military installations, or anything that might be construed as 'sensitive'. In Syria, the definition of 'sensitive' can include bridges and very unimportant public buildings, which may have an armed guard at the entrance.

Safety

Syria is probably the safest of all the Middle Eastern countries in which to travel. Nevertheless, the usual precautions are advisable with regard to valuables: never leave them unattended in hotel rooms, and keep your money and important documents (passport, etc) on your person, preferably in a money-belt or something similar.

Travel to Syria: security update

The Syrian uprising began on March 18 2011 when the arrest of several local children, detained for spray-painting anti-government slogans along the wall of their school, sparked a demonstration for their release in the southern border town of Deraa about a 1½ hour's drive from the capital. When security forces stepped in and responded violently to quell the protest, unrest swept across Syria with many other towns also becoming hotspots of dissent. Although so far central Damascus has seen relatively few demonstrations, and has overall remained a pocket of calm, outlying suburbs such as Harasta have seen some localised protests and violent clashes between civilians and the military. There is a large police presence in the city and road blocks and police checkpoints are now common on all roads into the capital and within certain areas.

The FCO currently advises against all travel to Syria, including Damascus, due to the unpredictable nature of the security situation. If you do decide to visit, you should exercise extreme vigilance with your safety and heed FCO advice to stay away from large gatherings, especially on Fridays which have seen the largest outbreaks of violence. All visitors should carry their passport with them at all times and be extra cautious when pointing their camera at anything that isn't an obvious tourist attraction. All foreign journalists have been expelled from the country and the security forces are suspicious of anyone wielding a camera.

Lone women may encounter minor hassle, though it almost always consists of nothing more than constant offers of marriage and is usually easily ignored. If you do find yourself being harassed don't be afraid to call for assistance. Most Syrians are appalled by this behaviour and will quickly come to your aid.

Probably the biggest danger tourists face is on the roads. Syrian driving is erratic, to say the least, and you need to keep a close eye on traffic (not to mention pedestrians, donkeys and a whole host of other dangers) when using the roads. When crossing a busy road as a pedestrian, use your right hand, to make the hand signal for 'astena' ('wait' in Arabic): bring the tip of your thumb to meet in the middle of the tips of your fingers and show this hand gesture to oncoming traffic. Surprisingly, this is actually extremely effective at stopping traffic. Syrian drivers like to speed. If you've hired a driver never be afraid to tell him to slow down or stop if you're not comfortable. The best advice if you're driving on Syrian roads is to practise defensive driving and always be aware of what might be coming up further along the road.

Taxes
Airport departure tax
At the time of research, people departing the country by air are still being charged the hefty airport departure tax of S£1500 but there is talk of phasing this out in the near future. Check with your hotel for up-to-date information.

Land departure tax
Departure tax is S£500 if you are leaving via a land border into Jordan or Lebanon and S£550 via the Bab al-Hawa border into Turkey.

Other taxes

Most top-end hotels add a 10% government tax to the room rate. Expensive restaurants also usually add 10% service tax to your bill.

Telephone

To call Syria from overseas dial your international access code, followed by Syria's country code **963** and then the area/town code (dropping the 0). To call an international phone number from within Syria dial **00**, followed by the country code.

Time

Syria is 2 hrs ahead of GMT Oct-Apr, and 3 hrs ahead May-Sep.

Tipping

Tipping is very much a way of life in Syria. In restaurants 10% is acceptable though remember that the more expensive restaurants often add a service charge anyway. Any person who provides a service (driver, guide, hotel porter) will expect a tip and what you give them is really down to your own discretion.

Tourist information

Syria does not have any dedicated tourist offices abroad, although their embassies can provide you with a selection of the Ministry of Tourism's free maps/pamphlets. All main towns and tourist centres have a tourist information office which hand out the free Ministry of Tourism maps. Staff are always friendly and willing to help but usually don't have much information. The Ministry of Tourism's website (see below) has some useful information and a handy calendar of events.

Useful websites

www.fco.gov.uk Homepage of the British Foreign and Commonwealth Office; gives current safety recommendations regarding travel in Syria.

www.newsfromsyria.com Excellent website with up-to-date news from the country.
www.syriatourism.org Official website of Syria's Ministry of Tourism.
www.whatsonsyria.com Web version of the free monthly magazine with events listings and lots of useful information for visitors.

Visas and immigration
Syrian visas

For detailed and up-to-date information on applying for a Syrian visa, contact your nearest Syrian embassy (see above for contact details of Syrian embassies abroad). All foreign nationals, except for nationals of Arab countries, require a visa to enter Syria. Your passport must be valid for at least 6 months beyond your intended stay.
Note Anyone whose passport shows evidence of a trip to Israel is not allowed into the country.
Single entry tourist visas are valid for 3 months from the date of issue and allow for a stay of up to 15 days. **Multiple entry** visas are valid for 6 months from the date of issue but again only allow for a stay of 15 days. Visa costs vary by nationality, check with the Syrian embassy for details.

In nearly all cases the tourist visa must be obtained before arriving in Syria. The only official exceptions to this rule are for nationalities that do not have a Syrian embassy in their country (eg New Zealanders and Dutch). These nationalities are entitled to a visa at the point of entry. In practice though, in the past couple of years, it has also been possible for Australians to be issued visas on arrival in Syria despite there being a Syrian embassy in Australia. This really all depends on the whims of the immigration officials at your time of entry and the best rule is for you to apply for your visa beforehand if you have a Syrian embassy in your home country.

Applying for a Syrian visa in a neighbouring country has become decidedly tricky in recent years. The Syrian embassy in Turkey is the only embassy that is still officially issuing visas to non-residents. Foreigners can apply at either the consulate in Istanbul or the embassy in Ankara. Visas take 1 working day to be processed and you will need to bring along a letter of recommendation from your country's embassy in Turkey, which you will most likely be charged a hefty fee for. Please be aware that some countries embassies refuse to supply letters of recommendation. Officially you can only apply for a Syrian visa in Jordan if you don't have a Syrian embassy in your home country, though in practice even if this is the case, you may be turned away and told to get your visa on the border. The Syrian embassy in Egypt has also stopped processing visas for foreigners, though there is always the odd exception to the rule that succeeds in getting one. As there is no Syrian embassy in Lebanon it is impossible to apply for a visa from there.

Visa extensions (of up to 2 months) are easily obtained once in Syria from any office of the Immigration and Passport Department, which have a branch in most main towns. Don't bother applying for an extension until your 14th day or you will most likely be told to come back again. Processing of extensions can usually be done on the same day and you will have to supply about 6 passport-sized photographs and a letter from your hotel. The cost of the extension varies from office to office but is always minimal. In general it is usually easier and faster to apply for an extension in any town other than Damascus (the offices in Tartus, Lattakia and Hama are particularly efficient).

Immigration

On arrival in Syria you have to fill out an **entry/exit card**. Keep this with you at all times throughout your trip in Syria as when you leave the country you will be asked to hand it in.

Weights and measures

The metric system is used in Syria.

Damascus

Damascus

Most of the city's sights are concentrated in the Old City and, if you have limited time, this is where you should focus your sightseeing. The various monuments are described below in as near as possible a logical order, but when exploring the Old City it is not really possible to conduct a detailed tour without a considerable amount of doubling back on yourself. ▸ *For listings, see pages 52-62.*

Ins and outs

Getting there and away

Damascus is Syria's major transport hub with frequent connections stretching to all major centres in the country by public transport. There are also bus services to Jordan, Lebanon and Turkey from here. Microbuses ply the routes between the city and the small surrounding towns (such as Maaloula), which the bigger buses don't service.

Damascus International Airport is roughly 30 km to the southeast of the city centre and handles the vast majority of international flights arriving in Syria as well as frequent domestic flights to Aleppo and Lattakia and a few per week to Qamishle and Deir ez-Zor. There is a taxi-stand inside the airport terminal. A taxi to the city centre will cost about S£700, but if you arrive late at night you may be charged more.

The city has two major bus stations. The Harasta Pullman Bus Station services all destinations to the north of Damascus including transport from Turkey, while the Al-Samariyeh Bus Station has connections to all the destinations to the south, including Jordan and Lebanon. Both terminals are out of the city centre. A taxi from either to the centre should cost around S£90.

All trains arrive into Kadem Station. There are good connections to Aleppo and daily services from Lattakia, Tartus, Deir-ez Zor, Hassakeh and Qameshli. There is a friendly and helpful information desk here. A taxi from the station into the city centre will cost about S£70. ▸ *See also transport on page 58.*

Getting around

Damascus is a relatively compact city, and for the most part walking is the best way to get around (in the Old City it is really the only way). Taxis are plentiful and cheap (S£30-40 for trips within the city centre) and therefore a convenient way to get between districts, or to/from the bus and train stations. These days, most have working meters; but if not, agree on a fare before setting off. The microbuses ('*meecro*' or '*servees*'), which zip all over the city, are difficult to get to grips with unless you can read Arabic, though certain routes can be useful.

One of the main terminals for microbuses is under Assad Bridge. There are services from here to the Harasta Pullman bus station as well as to Abbasseen and Mezzeh. Journeys cost S£5-10. Bear in mind that they cannot really accommodate large items of luggage, although you can always try paying for two seats.

Orientation

Although modern-day Damascus spreads over a large area, its core is surprisingly compact. The Old City comprises a distinct area, enclosed within city walls which, for the most part, still survive. Immediately to the northwest of this is the main centre of the modern city. Here, Martyrs' Square (in Arabic 'al-Marjeh', but also known as Al-Shouhada Square) is the focus for many of the cheap hotels and restaurants (this is also Damascus' 'red-light' district).

Running west from the Citadel, which is situated at the northwest corner of the Old City, An Naser Street takes you past the Hejaz railway station, terminus for the famous Hejaz railway line, from where a major north-south axis runs along Said al-Jabri, Port Said and 29 May streets passing through the main commercial and business centre of the city. Intersecting this north-south axis is another major east-west axis, Shoukri al-Kouwatli Street.

Heading west, this takes you past the Tekkiyeh as-Suleimaniyeh complex and the National Museum, separated from the main road by a branch of the Barada River, before reaching Umawiyeen 'Square' (in fact a huge roundabout).

Just west of the National Museum the large Assad Bridge crosses Shoukri al-Kouwatli Street. Following it north and then northwest leads you up into the modern, fashionable

1 Damascus overview

➡ Damascus maps
1 Damascus overview, page 21
2 Damascus centre, page 28
3 Damascus Old City, page 30
4 Umayyad Mosque, page 35

500 metres
500 yards

Abu Roumaneh district where many of the foreign embassies are located. Further north still, the long ridge of Kassioun mountain dominates the skyline, with the ancient districts of Salihiye/Al-Charkasiye, once separated from the old city by countryside, strung out along its lower slopes.

Extending southwest from Umawiyeen Square, meanwhile, is the modern district of Al-Mezzeh, strung out along the busy thoroughfare of Fayez Mansour Street. This newly affluent area of Damascus also houses a number of foreign embassies.

Tourist information

Main Tourist office ① *29 May St, T011-232 3953, www.syriantourism.org, Sat-Thu 0930-1900.* The staff on duty are friendly but the most information you'll get is a free map and some pamphlets. They have a habit of running out of English-language maps at this office but seem to have a huge stock of German- and French-language ones.

There's also a **Tourist Information Counter** ① *at the airport, open 24 hrs in theory but often unattended,* and a little **tourist office** ① *at the entrance to the Handicrafts Market, just off Omar Ben Abi Rabeea St, daily 0900-1900 (approx).* The staff here are ultra-friendly and seem to be more switched on with information.

Background

Earliest stages

The setting of Damascus is the key to its historical importance, and that a permanent settlement should develop here is no surprise. The Barada river, flowing down from the Anti-Lebanon mountains to the northeast, waters the *Ghouta* plain below and has created a large, fertile oasis on the edge of an otherwise harsh and inhospitable desert stretching south and east. Over the centuries, Damascus has continually found itself at an important strategic and commercial crossroads.

It is precisely because Damascus has been inhabited continuously throughout its long history that there is very little physical evidence of the earliest stages of its settlement. Each successive civilization has built over the foundations of the one which proceeded it. Excavations in the Old City and at Tel as-Salihiye to the east have nevertheless revealed evidence of settlement during the fourth and third millenniums BC respectively. Our knowledge of the early history of the city, however, comes primarily from fragmentary literary sources.

Amongst the large numbers of tablets discovered at Mari, some, which date back to 2500 BC, make reference to Damascus (then known as *Dimashqa*), while slightly later tablets from Ebla make reference to *Dimaski*, although its exact relationship with these important city-states is far from clear.

Ancient empires

From around 2000 BC Damascus was settled by the **Amorites**, one of the many waves of Semitic peoples to migrate from the desert interior of the Arabian peninsula and settle in the fertile lands further north. Some 500 years later, the city came under **Egyptian** influence during the rule of Thutmosis III, as recorded in the Amarna tablets. In turn it then came under the control of the other great regional power of the time, the **Hittites**.

Sometime after 1200 BC the **Aramaeans** established themselves in the city, and from the 10th to eighth centuries BC *Aram Damascus* was the seat of an important Aramaean kingdom. It was during this period that the Temple of Haddad was built on the site of what is now the Umayyad Mosque. The Aramaeans clashed repeatedly with the biblical kingdoms of Israel and Judah, limiting their northward expansion, as chronicled at length in the Old Testament. At the same time, the Aramaeans came under repeated attack from the growing **Assyrian** Empire in northern Mesopotamia, and finally in 732 BC the city was devastated by the Assyrian king, Tiglath Pileser III. The **Babylonians** followed in 572 BC, led by King Nebuchadnezzar, and the **Achaemenid Persians** in 539 BC, under King Cyrus.

Greek and Roman eras

Following the defeat of the Persians by the **Greeks** at the battle of Issus, one of Alexander the Great's generals, Parmenion, captured Damascus in 332 BC and it was under subsequent Greek rule that a planned grid pattern of development was first applied to the city.

With the death of Alexander the Great in 323 BC, Damascus then found itself caught for two centuries between the competing ambitions of the **Seleucid** and **Ptolemid** Empires. However, decline in the influence of both left the door open to the **Nabateans** who, under Aretas III (84-56 BC), extended their empire to include Damascus.

The first **Roman** conquest of Syria came as early as 64 BC, but Damascus at that point remained of peripheral importance, with Nabatean control over what was effectively a semi-independent city-state continuing until as late as AD 54. Thus events such as the conversion of St Paul in the early years of Christianity took place before direct Roman control had been established. However, in the first century AD the Romans took direct control of Damascus and from that point onwards it grew in importance. In AD 117 the Emperor Hadrian declared it a metropolis, and in AD 222 Severus raised its status to that of a colony. Trade across what was now a relatively stable Roman Empire flourished, and Damascus reaped the rewards of being an important centre at the junction of major caravan routes.

There was a characteristically Roman flurry of building activity during this period. A *castrum* on the site of the citadel was established. The city walls were strengthened and gates were installed. The Temple of Haddad was expanded and embellished to become the Temple of Jupiter. The Via Recta (Straight Street) was widened and colonnaded to create the *decumanus maximus* and aqueducts were built; adding to the system of irrigation first developed by the Aramaeans to harness the waters of the Barada.

Byzantine Damascus

During the **Byzantine** era (from the fourth century AD) Christianity became firmly established in the city. The Temple of Jupiter was converted into a church dedicated to St John the Baptist and Damascus became the seat of a bishopric, second only to the patriarchate in Antioch. However, the Byzantine Empire found itself under constant threat from the **Sassanid Persians** and eventually in AD 612 Damascus was briefly occupied by them, before being regained by Heraclius in AD 628.

The Islamic empire's capital

This brief incursion by the Sassanids was the prelude to a far more permanent transition brought about by the expansion of the **Islamic** Empire of the nomadic tribes of the

Arabian peninsula following the death of their Prophet Muhammad. Led by Khalid Ibn al-Walid, the Muslim army first took Damascus in AD 635, withdrawing to defeat Heraclius in the decisive battle of Yarmouk before occupying the city permanently in AD 636. Under this new regime, Damascus was at first a relatively unimportant outpost of an Islamic Empire whose political centre was Medina. However, in AD 661 the governor of Damascus, Mu'awiya, assumed the title of Caliph, initiating the **Umayyad** Dynasty and making Damascus the new capital of the Islamic Empire. For Syria, and particularly Damascus, this resulted in a great cultural flowering, most eloquently and enduringly expressed in the architecture of the Umayyad Mosque.

Umayyad rule lasted for nearly a hundred years until in AD 750 a new dynasty, that of the **Abbasids**, was established. Damascus was replaced by Baghdad as the capital of the Islamic Empire, and fell into decline. The unity of the now huge Islamic Empire began to give way to competing spheres of influence centred on Baghdad, Cairo, Mosul and Aleppo, with Damascus caught between them. From the ninth century it came under the control of the **Tulunids**, **Ikshidids** and **Fatimids** of Egypt, before passing in 1076 to the **Seljuk Turks** who had by then expanded from their capital at Isfahan to take control of both Aleppo and Mosul.

Seljuk rule was in an advanced state of decline by the time the **Crusaders** arrived in the 12th century. However, despite coming under attack three times in the first half of the century, Damascus was never taken by the Crusaders. Nur ud-Din, the **Zengid** ruler of Aleppo, assumed control of the city in 1154, and was followed by Salah ud-Din in 1174, who by that time had overthrown the Fatimids of Egypt to establish the **Ayyubid** Dynasty. Together, Nur ud-Din and Salah ud-Din led the Muslim resistance to the Crusaders and Damascus flourished once again as an important political centre.

The first **Mongol** invasion of 1260 brought devastation to Damascus and an abrupt end to Ayyubid rule. However the **Mamluk** Dynasty of Egypt quickly came to the rescue, defeating the Mongols and establishing their rule in Syria. Damascus flourished yet again, particularly under the rule of Baibars (1260-1277) and later under the governorship of Tengiz (1312-1339), becoming a second capital after Cairo and witnessing another burst of building activity. The Mongol threat continued, however, and after repelling an attack in 1299-1300, the city was largely destroyed by the Mongol leader Tamerlane in 1400. Although Mamluk rule was restored, the city never fully recovered under them.

Ottoman era

In 1516 the **Ottoman Turks**, led by Selim I, took Damascus and incorporated Syria into their huge empire. The Ottoman's control and protection of the *Hajj* (pilgrimage to Mecca) helped reinforce their claim to the Caliphate, and throughout their 400 years of rule Damascus was of central importance as the last great staging post on the annual pilgrimage. Inevitably for such a large empire, the city's governors enjoyed a large degree of independence. Indeed, the first Pasha of Damascus, **Al-Ghazali**, declared himself independent of Ottoman rule and the city suffered considerable damage when it was retaken by the armies of Suleiman I in 1521.

Later pashas exercised their independence more cautiously. Amongst the **Azem** family, who between themselves ruled for most of the 18th century, Darwish Pasha, Murad Pasha and most notably Assad Pasha were competent governors who did much to improve the city. However, corruption and stagnation began to set in and when

Muhammad Ali, the Pasha of Cairo, rose against Ottoman rule in 1805, Damascus soon followed suit and control of the city passed to Muhammad Ali's son **Ibrahim** Pasha in 1832. His rule lasted until 1840 and saw a brief burst of civic improvements but the return to direct Ottoman rule also saw a return to stagnation. In 1860, clashes between Christian and Druze minorities in Lebanon spread to Damascus and culminated in a massacre of Christians living in the city, the Christians having maintained a minimal presence here since the Byzantine era. **Midhat** Pasha brought further civic improvements towards the end of the 19th century, and at the same time Damascus, with its large concentration of intellectuals, became a centre of Arab nationalism.

The French mandate and road to independence
When the Ottoman Turks allied with the Germans at the start of the First World War, Damascus became yet again an important strategic centre and its fall to the Allied forces in 1918 heralded the fall of the Ottoman Empire. The Arab nationalist dream of an independent Syria was briefly recognized under the leadership of **Feisal**, who had been central to the Arab revolt upon which the Allies had relied so heavily. However, in the superpower carve-up that inevitably followed, this was replaced by French Mandate rule in 1920 and Damascus became for a while the capital of a mini-state. In 1925 an uprising against the French resulted in the bombing of Damascus which caused considerable damage, but it was not until 1945 that the city became the capital of an independent Syrian Arab Republic.

Modern Damascus
Today Damascus is a sprawling metropolis with all the trappings of a modern capital and Syria's major commercial and government hub. Like all large cities in the region it struggles with the problems of traffic, pollution and coping with an ever-expanding population caused by rural to urban drift in the last 50 years. This has been exacerbated recently by the huge number of Iraqi refugees who have flooded into Damascus since the Iraq war.

At the time of going to press, the FCO is advising against all travel to Syria. See box on page 15 for more details.

Sights

Citadel

ⓘ *Officially closed to the public and only opened up for concerts, but the north-side entrance is usually left open and nobody seems to mind if you wander in and have a look.*

The Citadel is an imposing structure standing at the northwest corner of the Old City, its massive western wall facing directly onto the modern thoroughfare of Ath Thawra Street. At the time of writing, it was undergoing extensive restoration – a painfully slow process which has been going on for more than 10 years – and closed to visitors. However you can view its walls from the outside and get some insight into the different stages of its tumultuous history. If you're in Damascus during one of the city's festivals (such as the Silk Road Festival) you may be lucky enough to gain access. The citadel is opened up and used to stage all of the city's major events.

Background

The site appears to have been utilized as a *castrum* or military camp during Roman times, probably during the reign of Diocletian, AD 284-305. Then, during the Byzantine and early Islamic periods, it was expanded to occupy roughly its present extent. After that there are no clear references to it until the Seljuk period (1058-1157) when a new fortress was constructed. After Salah ud-Din took control of Damascus in 1174 he strengthened it, adding a tower, and it became an important centre for his military operations. Most of what can be seen today, however, dates from the 13th century.

Under threat from both the Crusader attack and local Syrian intrigues, Al-Adil, brother of Salah ud-Din and successor to the Ayyubid leadership, set about building a new citadel in 1202. Work continued until well after his death, with new walls and towers being constructed along with a palace complex and mosque. In 1260 the great Mongol invasions from the east reached Damascus and the citadel was largely destroyed. It was subsequently rebuilt by the Mamluk Sultan Baibars, only to be attacked again by the Mongols in the 1300, and then destroyed by Tamerlane in 1400. During the Ottoman period the citadel was partially repaired but its importance declined and it gradually fell into disuse. Following Syrian independence, it was used once again as a barracks, and then later as a prison before work started on its restoration as a historic monument.

Tour of the citadel walls

Facing the western wall of the citadel from Ath Thawra Street, the whole of the southwest tower along with the curtain wall up to the small central gate is an obviously modern reconstruction. The new stonework is rather too neat and crisp perhaps, but it gives a good idea of the full proportions of the massive, solid southwest tower. This tower has carried the full brunt of sieges, fires and earthquakes over the centuries; since Al-Adil first built it in roughly its present form at the start of the 13th century, it has been destroyed and rebuilt no less than six times.

The remainder of the western wall has also been largely reconstructed, but this time using old stones from the Ayyubid and Mamluk periods. Various recycled architectural fragments bearing inscriptions and insignia can be seen in the upper parts of these walls.

At eye level, just to the right of the central gate, there is one interesting block carved with a dragon and rosette (though unfortunately placed upside-down, making it a little difficult to identify as such). Note also the recently discovered and only partially reconstructed tower to the right of the main gate, thought to be one of two flanking it, which were built by Baibars but destroyed in an earthquake in 1759 and never rebuilt. The large metal statue of a mounted soldier in flowing gown that stands by the main gate is of Salah ud-Din.

The northwest tower shows evidence of various different stages of construction and reconstruction in its stonework, from the Ayyubid through to the Ottoman periods. When Baibars restored the citadel, he had a belvedere built on top of this tower, from where he would review his troops and hold audiences.

From the corner of the northwest tower, you can follow the small cobbled street that runs between the Barada River and the northern wall (this also makes a pleasant alternative to Hamidiyeh Souq as a way of reaching the Umayyad Mosque and surrounding areas). The stonework you see is entirely of Mamluk origin (with later reconstructions), Baibars having built a new wall some 10 m in front of Al-Adil's. You first pass a small squat tower with an inscription on the north face commemorating its reconstruction in 1508. The street then passes under an arch with an inscription above it. Once through the arch you are in fact inside the remains of another tower, rebuilt according to the inscription by Nawruz al-Haifizi in 1407. Further on is a rectangular tower with just a very small central entrance and three arrow slits in the walls. You come next to the northeast corner tower which shows evidence of repeated repair and reconstruction. Turning right, you can see in the east wall of the tower an Arabic inscription in an elaborate frame; the inscription names Al-Adil as the builder of the tower, although it was probably taken from another tower and re-used here during later repair and reconstruction work. From here you can visit the nearby gate to the Old City, Bab al-Faraj, and work your way along the northern section of the city walls, taking in also Bab al-Faradis, Bab as-Salaam and Bab Touma (see page 43).

Following the eastern wall southwards there are various fragments of inscriptions in it, followed by a long rectangular tower and then the large central gateway, today largely obscured by modern buildings. The remainder of the east wall, along with the whole of the south wall parallel with Hamidiyeh Souq, are likewise obscured.

Old City

The Old City, retaining so much of its long and varied history, is certainly Damascus' greatest attraction. As soon as you step into it, you are drawn into a completely different, medieval world, only brought back to the present by the ringing horns of cars, trying to navigate the narrow lanes. From Saturday to Thursday you'll find yourself being swept along by the crowds of shoppers scouring the ancient souqs for bargains or the shrouded groups of pilgrims threading their way through the streets to visit another sight. Visit on Friday morning and you'll find a different world, with most of the city silent and shut down.

Around practically every corner you will find another beautiful and atmospheric historic monument. Such immediate history might become overwhelming were it not for the fact that so many of these monuments are still in use, set firmly in the context of a living city.

Hamidiyeh Souq

This is the best way to enter the Old City for the first time, taking you through a colourful and lively souq directly to the Umayyad Mosque. This is a thoroughly Syrian market, and while travellers might hunt around for antique silver jewellery or Bedouin carpets, there are more people shopping for everyday items such as fabric, clothes, kitchen utensils, etc.

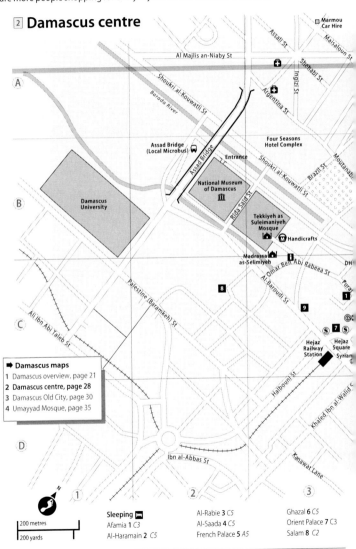

2 Damascus centre

➡ Damascus maps
1 Damascus overview, page 21
2 **Damascus centre, page 28**
3 Damascus Old City, page 30
4 Umayyad Mosque, page 35

Sleeping
Afamia **1** C3
Al-Haramain **2** C5

Al-Rabie **3** C5
Al-Saada **4** C5
French Palace **5** A5

Ghazal **6** C5
Orient Palace **7** C3
Salam **8** C2

In its present form the souq dates from the late 19th century, when the governor of Damascus, Rashid Nasha Pasha, modified the existing Souq al-Jadid by widening and straightening it, constructing two-storey shops along its length and erecting the corrugated-iron roofing. On completion, it was named after the Ottoman Sultan, Abdel Hamid II. History has taken its toll on the corrugated-iron roofing: the holes which pepper

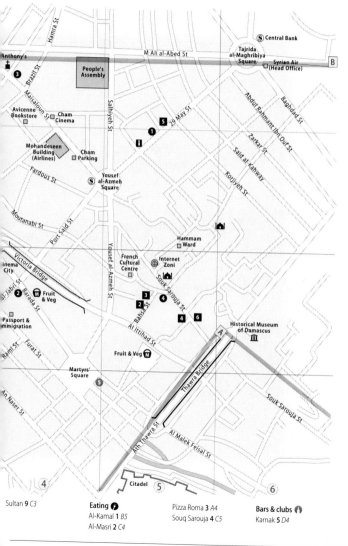

it were the result of the triumphant rifle shots of the Arab forces who rode into the city in the wake of the Ottoman and German retreat of 1917 and, later, the machine-gun fire rained down by French planes during the Druze rebellion of 1925.

As you approach the end of Hamadiyeh Souq, you get a glimpse of the towering, majestic southwest minaret of the Umayyad Mosque. At the same time, the remains of a **Roman Propylaeum** or monumental gateway (often mistakenly referred to as a

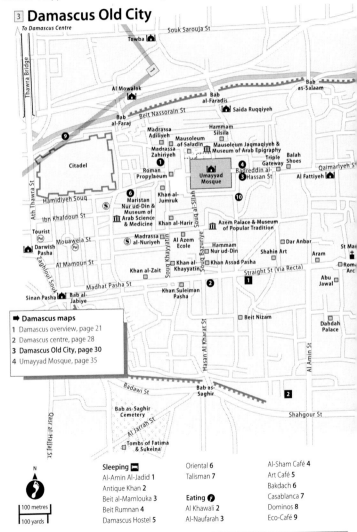

3 Damascus Old City

To Damascus Centre
Souk Sarouja St
Towba
Thawra Bridge
Al Mowalak
Bab al-Faradis
Bab as-Salaam
Bab al-Faraj
Beit Nassorain St
Saida Ruqqiyeh
Citadel
Madrassa Adiliyeh
Mausoleum of Saladin
Hammam Silsila
Madrassa Zahiriyeh
Mausoleum Jaqmaqiyeh & Museum of Arab Epigraphy
Balah Shoes
Qaimariyeh S
Ath Thawra St
Roman Propylaeum
Umayyad Mosque
Triple Gateway
Badreddin al-Hassan St
Al Fattiyeh
Hamidiyeh Souq
Khan al-Jumruk
Maristan Nur ud-Din & Museum of Arab Science & Medicine
Ibn Khaldoun St
Khan al-Harir
Azem Palace & Museum of Popular Tradition
Dar Anbar
St Ma
Tourist
Mouaweia St
Darwish Pasha
Madrassa al-Nuriyeh
Al Azem Ecole
Hammam Nur ud-Din
Shahin Art
Aram
Rom Arc
Al Mamoun St
Khan al-Zait
Khan al-Khayyatin
Khan Assad Pasha
Straight St (Via Recta)
Abu Jawal
Madhat Pasha St
Khan Suleiman Pasha
Sinan Pasha
Bab al-Jabiye
Beit Nizam
Dahdah Palace
Hasan Al Kharat St
Al Amin St
Badawi St
Bab as-Saghir
Qasr al-Hajjar St
Bab as-Saghir Cemetery
Al Jarrah St
Tombs of Fatima & Sukeina
Shahgour St

N
100 metres
100 yards

Sleeping 🛏
Al-Amin Al-Jadid 1
Antique Khan 2
Beit al-Mamlouka 3
Beit Rumnan 4
Damascus Hostel 5

Oriental 6
Talisman 7

Eating 🍴
Al Khawali 2
Al-Naufarah 3

Al-Sham Café 4
Art Café 5
Bakdach 6
Casablanca 7
Dominos 8
Eco-Café 9

triumphal arch) appear in front of you, marking the end of the souq. To the left are two huge free-standing columns and capitals, while to the right, three equally large columns and capitals support a segment of the original massive semi- circular arch, framed within a triangular pediment, which would once have extended across six columns. The *propylaeum* marks the outer gateway at the western end of the Temple of Jupiter which once stood on the present site of the Umayyad Mosque (see below). The Temple would originally have been approached from the east side, so that this *propylaeum* was in fact primarily an exit and the decoration is therefore on the inside. The best way to view the Roman remains is from the mosque side; from here you can see the true scale of the arch as well as the intricate decoration that adorns it.

Running at right angles to the *propylaeum* are the remains of an arcade, in fact a Byzantine shopping complex dating from around AD 330-340. Today, various Koran sellers can be found plying their trade along its length. Beyond this, you come out into an open square, cleared in recent years of the numerous shops and stalls that once filled the area. In front of you is the towering west wall of the Umayyad Mosque, 150 m in length and rising to over 100 m. Its stonework contains in it a record of the various historical phases, from the large-block lower courses of Roman origin, through the smaller stones of early Arab/Muslim times, to the occasional patches of modern restoration.

Umayyad Mosque

① *The ticket office is through a small gate to the left of the mosque's main entrance, signposted 'putting on special clothes room'. The usual tourist entrance is via the north gate (Bab al-Amara) which you access through the gardens, past the Mausoleum of Salah ud-Din. At the time of writing the gardens were a messy building site and tourists were being allowed to enter through the main gate in the west wall, Bab al-Barid, after buying their tickets. Open daily for tourists, except Fri 1230-1400 when it's closed for main prayers. Non-Muslims S£50 (includes entry to Mausoleum of Salah ud-Din). Women must wear the provided abeyyas and men not dressed modestly (knees showing) will have to wear a long skirt. Shoes must be taken off before entering the mosque and are carried with you (a small bag is handy for this).*

However many times you visit the Umayyad Mosque, the impact of this awe-inspiring building remains undiminished. If anything, it grows on you with every visit, and once you have paid due attention to the various architectural details, you are free to let the overall effect and atmosphere slowly soak in. And for all its grandeur and religious importance (it is one of the great holy sites of Islam after Mecca, Medina and the Dome of the Rock in Jerusalem), it is in no way a sombre place. Quite the contrary: gangs of young children run around the courtyard laughing and playing freely while families and groups of worshippers come and go; the scale and calm and beauty of the place easily absorbing and embracing the throng of human activity while never oppressing it. Here you can leave behind the crowds and congestion of Damascus and enter another world altogether, one which still manages to maintain a connection with the human and the ordinary, while at the same time somehow lifting it up into another level of significance.

Background
The Umayyad Mosque stands on a site of religious importance dating back to the second millennium BC. At this time a temple to Hadad, the **Aramaean** god of rain and fertility, and his consort Atargatis, existed here, although little is known about its exact form or extent. These gods came in time to be identified with the **Roman** gods Jupiter and Venus, and under Roman patronage the temple was expanded in the first century AD and then further embellished under the reign of Septimus Severus (AD 193-211), becoming known in the process as the Temple of Jupiter. The inner enclosure or *temenos* of the temple corresponded approximately with the walls of the present mosque and within this would have been the *cella* or central shrine. Surrounding the *temenos* was a much larger outer courtyard marked by a portico pierced by four gateways, traces of which still survive in the western *propylaeum* (see above) and also in the eastern triple-arched *propylaeum* and the column bases to the north of it (see below).

With the adoption of Christianity as the official religion of the Roman Empire (the point which also marks the start of the **Byzantine** era), the Temple of Jupiter was converted into a Christian church and dedicated to St John the Baptist, most probably during the reign of Emperor Theodosius (AD 379-395), who is thought to have ordered the destruction of the pagan shrine in the first year of his rule. In AD 636, following the defeat of the Byzantine forces of Heraclius at the Battle of Yarmouk, the Arab armies of Islam took Damascus. Initially, Christians continued to worship in the church, sharing the huge compound with Muslims who built a small *mihrab* in the south wall, which faced in the direction of Mecca.

However in AD 661, under the **Umayyad** Dynasty, Damascus became the capital of the Islamic Empire and with this shift, pressure increased for a purely Muslim place of worship. It was under the Umayyad Caliph Khalid Ibn al-Walid that the huge compound was finally appropriated and work started on an Islamic mosque on a grand scale in AD 708. The enterprise was an enormous one, which suffered various setbacks and entailed massive expenditure, but the end result was the greatest monument to Islam of that period.

Over the centuries the mosque has survived invasions, sackings, earthquakes and fires, although with each calamity it has undergone a transformation of one sort or another.

Khalid Ibn al-Walid and the Umayyad Mosque

The Umayyad period brought with it a great flowering of architectural expression in Syria, drawing inspiration from the rich Byzantine, Persian, Mesopotamian and local influences which existed at the time. Khalid Ibn al-Walid, the sixth Umayyad Caliph, was famous in particular for his architectural enterprises. He was responsible for the building of the Al-Aqsa mosque in Jerusalem, and for the Great Mosque in Medina.

Al-Walid ordered work to start on the building of the Umayyad Mosque in Damascus in AD 708. The project lasted for seven years, reaching completion in AD 715, the same year as his death. Thousands of craftsmen were brought in from Constantinople and Egypt to work alongside the Syrian craftsmen. Originally, practically every surface was covered with mosaics, including the whole of the floor of the courtyard. Inside the prayer hall, 600 gold lanterns hung from the ceilings, while all the column capitals were plated with gold.

According to one account, it cost the state's entire revenue throughout this period. Another account relates how 400 chests each containing 14,000 dinars were needed to pay for the work, and that a total of 18 camels were needed to bring the receipts to Al-Walid, who had them burnt without even looking at them, saying: "We spent this for Allah and shall make no account of it."

The most devastating, and most recent calamity, came in 1893 when a fire largely destroyed the prayer hall. Restoration, involving the replacement of the interior columns and central dome, was undertaken by the Ottomans, although much of the original decoration and beauty were lost in the process. However, for all that, and perhaps because of the amalgam of different influences and modifications over the centuries, today the Umayyad Mosque stands out as an exceptionally beautiful monument.

Visiting the mosque

The courtyard   The northern **Bab al-Amara** gate brings you into the courtyard of the mosque, with the prayer hall and its striking mosaic-covered central transept in front of you. The **courtyard**, measuring over 50 m by 120 m, is a huge open space paved with white marble slabs. These date from the late 19th-century restoration, which followed the great fire of 1893. Their effect is quite striking, particularly in bright sunlight, although one can only imagine what it must have been like when the whole area was covered with mosaics.

Surrounding the courtyard on three sides is an **arcade**. Along the east and west sides of the courtyard the arcade retains its original pattern of two circular columns interspaced by a square pillar, the latter being newly clad in marble, while along the north side, except for a few columns at either end, all have been replaced over the centuries by square pillars and recently clad. The inside walls of the arcades have likewise been decorated with marble as part of ongoing restoration work. All three arcades are topped by a smaller upper-storey arcade of delicate columns and arches, with fragments of mosaic surviving in places.

In the centre of the courtyard there is an **ablution fountain** of recent origin and on either side of it are small columns topped by newly added metal globes, meant to hold lanterns. Towards the west end of the courtyard, supported on eight columns topped by ornate Corinthian capitals, is a large, mosaic-covered octagonal structure with a domed top. This is known as the **Dome of the Treasury** (*Khubbet al-Khazneh* or *Beit al-Hal*). The structure, as the name suggests, was the mosque's treasury. It is thought to have been built in AD 788 by the Abbasid governor of Damascus, Fadil Ibn Salih, although the columns and capitals on which it rests are clearly recycled from Roman times. The fine mosaic work itself, consisting of plant motifs in green and gold, probably dates from 13th- or 14th-century restoration work. Towards the eastern end of the courtyard there is a smaller structure of identical design, though without the mosaic work and built much later (18th or 19th century), popularly known as the **Dome of the Clocks**. Predictably enough, it was used to house the mosque's clock collection.

In the northeast corner of the mosque, a doorway leads through into the **Shrine of Hussein**. According to legend, the head of this Shi'ite martyr, killed at the Battle of Karbala, was brought here and placed in a niche by the Caliph Yazid as a way of humiliating the followers of Ali. Today the niche is fronted by a silver grille and has become an important place of pilgrimage for Shi'ites who come here in large numbers, although there are conflicting traditions as to the final resting place of his head.

Mosaics and minarets The most striking feature of the prayer hall from the outside is the façade of the central transept, which is covered in mosaics. It is by looking at these mosaics that you can best conjure up an idea of what the mosque originally looked like when almost every surface was likewise adorned. The mosaic work on the central transept consists largely of restoration carried out in the 1960s, with only the darker patches being original. The other area where sections of mosaic have been preserved and restored is along the western arcade. On the inside wall, towards the northern end, is a section known as the **Barada Panel**. The theory is that this is a depiction of the Barada River, lined with lush vegetation and enticing villas, as it was in ancient times, although it could equally represent a scene from Paradise. In the entrance hall, just inside **Bab al-Barid**, there are further elaborate mosaics which, like all the mosaics in the Umayyad Mosque, are notable for the complete absence of any human figures: such representations are considered blasphemous in Islamic tradition. The intricately painted wooden ceiling here (a restoration of the 15th-century original) is also particularly beautiful. Note also the huge bronze panelled wooden doors of the Bab al-Barid, which date from 1416. A good time to view the mosaics of the western arcade is in the evening when they are floodlit.

The mosque's three **minarets** can be viewed from different parts of the courtyard. Beside the Bab al-Amara in the centre of the northern wall is the **Minaret of the Bride**. The lower part dates from the ninth century, while the upper part was added in the late 12th century. According to a local story, its construction was originally financed by a merchant whose daughter was betrothed to the Caliph of the time, hence the name.

In the southwest corner is the **Minaret al-Gharbiye**, also known as the Minaret Qait Bey after the Mamluk Sultan who built it in 1488. It is particularly graceful and shows the strong Egyptian influence typical of the Mamluk period. In the southeast corner is the **Minaret of Jesus**, the tallest of the three. The main body is Ayyubid, dating from 1247 and replacing an Umayyad minaret, while the tip is Ottoman. According to Islamic belief, Jesus will descend from heaven to do battle with the Antichrist before the Day of Judgement, and according to local Damascene tradition, he will descend via this minaret. Both the southeast and southwest minarets are believed to have been built on the foundations of Roman towers, although some scholars have questioned this, pointing out that no other examples of Roman temples have towers at the corners.

The prayer hall The prayer hall occupies the whole of the southern length of the mosque, and basically follows a basilica plan, although the long, narrow, triple-aisled hall is broken by a central transept topped by a massive dome that serves to orientate worshippers towards the *mihrab* in the centre of the south wall. Some scholars suggest that the Muslim architects followed the plan of the existing Byzantine church, modifying it by adding the central transept, thus shifting the focus of the building away from the east wall where the altar would have been, to the *mihrab* in the centre of the south wall. However, there is no firm evidence to indicate the exact form or extent of the Byzantine church, and others argue that Al-Walid completely dismantled the church before starting work on the mosque. What you see today is largely the Ottoman reconstruction following the fire of 1893. Despite being in no way as elaborate as the original must have been, in its cavernous, cool, airy enormity it is still impressive. The floors are covered throughout with carpets, while numerous fans dangle from a huge height, wobbling as they spin.

In the central transept, the towering **Dome of the Eagle**, resting on four colossal pillars, is somewhat austere in its present form, though still awesome for its sheer size. Its name derives from the idea that the domed transept represents the head and body of an eagle, with the prayer hall extending to either side, representing the wings. As well as the main *mihrab* and *minbar* beside it, there are three other smaller *mihrabs* or niches, dedicated to

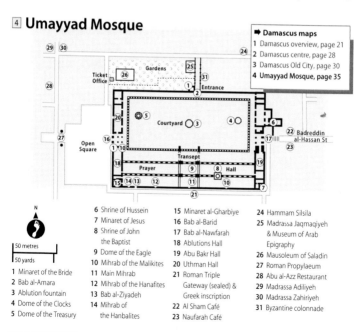

4 Umayyad Mosque

➡ **Damascus maps**
1 Damascus overview, page 21
2 Damascus centre, page 28
3 Damascus Old City, page 30
4 Umayyad Mosque, page 35

1 Minaret of the Bride
2 Bab al-Amara
3 Ablution fountain
4 Dome of the Clocks
5 Dome of the Treasury
6 Shrine of Hussein
7 Minaret of Jesus
8 Shrine of John
  the Baptist
9 Dome of the Eagle
10 Mihrab of the Malikites
11 Main Mihrab
12 Mihrab of the Hanafites
13 Bab al-Ziyadeh
14 Mihrab of
  the Hanbalites
15 Minaret al-Gharbiye
16 Bab al-Barid
17 Bab al-Nawfarah
18 Ablutions Hall
19 Abu Bakr Hall
20 Uthman Hall
21 Roman Triple
  Gateway (sealed) &
  Greek inscription
22 Al Sham Café
23 Naufarah Café
24 Hammam Silsila
25 Madrassa Jaqmaqiyeh
  & Museum of Arab
  Epigraphy
26 Mausoleum of Saladin
27 Roman Propylaeum
28 Abu al-Azz Restaurant
29 Madrassa Adiliyeh
30 Madrassa Zahiriyeh
31 Byzantine colonnade

the Hanbalites, Hanafites and Malikites, the three other schools of Sunni law besides the Shaffi school which was dominant in Damascus.

To the east of the central transept, encompassing two columns of the line nearest the south wall, is the **Shrine of John the Baptist**, consisting of an elaborate, dome-topped mausoleum made of marble. This dates from the Ottoman period, replacing an earlier wooden shrine which was destroyed in the fire of 1893. According to legend, during the building of the mosque, Al-Walid's workers discovered a casket buried underground containing the head of St John the Baptist, still with its hair and skin intact.

Mausoleum of Salah ud-Din

① Access through small gate to the left of the mosque's main entrance, signposted 'putting on special clothes room'. Just through the gate is the ticket office, at the end of the path on the left is the dome-topped building of the mausoleum. Daily 1000-1700, non-Muslims S£50 (includes mosque entry), women must wear an abeyya (available in the ticket office) and men wearing shorts will be given a long skirt to wear. At the entry to the mausoleum remove your shoes, no photography allowed.

For such a seminal figure in Arab history, the Mausoleum of Salah ud-Din is surprisingly small and unassuming. The dome-topped building dating from 1196, three years after the death of Salah ud-Din, originally stood within a larger *madrassa*, but nothing remains of this other than a solitary arch nearby. The mausoleum itself was in such an advanced state of disrepair by the end of the 19th century that when Kaiser Wilhelm II of Germany visited Damascus in 1898, he financed its restoration and donated a new tomb of white marble. Inside, the chamber is decorated with blue and white glazed tiles and bands of black, white and yellow stone. Alongside the white marble tomb donated by Wilhelm II is the original, a wooden one richly carved in black and gold and encased in glass.

Around the Umayyad Mosque

A little to the northwest of the Umayyad Mosque, facing each other across a narrow street, are the Madrassa Zahiriyeh and Madrassa Adiliyeh. Originally the **Madrassa Zahiriyeh** was the private house of Ayub, the father of Salah ud-Din. Following the death of the Mamluk Sultan Baibars in 1277, his son converted it into a religious school (*madrassa*), adding a mausoleum to house his father's body.

The recessed entrance, which dates from the building's conversion, is particularly imposing, consisting of contrasting black and yellow stonework, with three bands of marble above the level of the doorway carrying Arabic inscriptions and above these a finely executed semi-dome sculpted into intricate geometrical shapes. Today the building houses a library, but there is usually someone on hand to show you around and open up the mausoleum itself, which is kept locked.

Inside there is a small courtyard; the doorway immediately on the right leads into the mausoleum of Baibars, an ornately decorated, domed chamber which represents the main focus of interest. Opposite the entrance is a beautiful *mihrab* framed within strikingly patterned black and white marble. Each of the walls, themselves decorated with marble, contain two arched doorways, while running around the room is a wide band of lavish golden mosaic work in the same style as those of the Umayyad Mosque.

Construction work on the **Madrassa Adiliyeh** began towards the end of the 12th century, but it was left unfinished until the death of Sultan al-Adil Saif ud-Din (the brother of Salah ud-Din) in 1218, whereupon his son completed it to serve as the mausoleum of his father. The entrance, though impressive in its own right, is somewhat overshadowed by that of the Madrassa Zahiriyeh, while the mausoleum itself is a simple and unadorned domed chamber with broad arches in each wall. The remainder of the building, which consists of rooms arranged around a central courtyard, also houses a library.

Situated by the short colonnade leading to the northern Bab al-Amara gate of the Umayyad Mosque is **Madrassa Jaqmaqiyeh/Museum of Arab Epigraphy** ① *Wed-Mon 0900-1530, S£75, students S£5*, built by Jaqmaq al-Argunsawi, the Mamluk governor of Damascus from 1421-1422 and later king of Egypt from 1438-1452. This *madrassa* has an impressive entrance façade typical of the period, while the interior is also well preserved, housing a collection of Arab epigraphy, both in the form of carved inscriptions and some beautifully illuminated texts.

Continuing east from the entrance to the Madrassa Jaqmaqiyeh and then bearing right, you can weave your way through a series of narrow alleys to arrive on Badreddin al-Hassan Street, which runs east from the east gate of the Umayyad Mosque. But if instead you bear left and head north towards Bab al-Faradis, you pass on your right the **Saida Ruqqiyeh Mosque** ① *men and women have separate entrances, women will be given an abeyya to wear at entrance, men should not have knees or shoulders uncovered, shoes must be taken off before entering*. This Shi'ite mosque provides a complete contrast to anything else found in the Old City. For a start it was built in 1985. Its style, meanwhile, is entirely Iranian in inspiration (and indeed Iranian-built), as can be clearly seen from the distinctive onion-shaped dome. Inside, it is lavishly decorated with glazed tiles and copious amounts of marble, while the central dome is a dazzling mirror-mosaic. The overall effect is quite striking in its bright, fresh newness. It is also incredibly lively around evening prayers, thronging with families of Shi'ite pilgrims, mostly from Iran. The mosque stands on the site of a shrine to Lady Ruqqiyeh who died in AD 680 and was the daughter of Hussein, the great martyr of the Shi'ites. Hence its importance as a Shi'ite place of pilgrimage.

You can also skirt around the outside of the Umayyad Mosque by following its southern wall. You first pass Bab al-Ziada, which leads directly into the prayer hall. Further along, partially obscured by an electrical installation, there are the remains of a Roman triple gateway in the wall of the mosque. Originally, this served as the southern entrance into the inner temenos of the Roman temple. The Greek inscription on the central lintel (*"Thy Kingdom, O Christ, is an everlasting Kingdom, and Thy dominion endureth throughout all generations"*) clearly demonstrates that it remained in use during the Byzantine period, perhaps serving also as an entrance for both Christians and Muslims when they shared the temple compound during the early years of Islamic rule. However, with the construction of Al-Walid's mosque it was blocked up, since it interfered with the positioning of the central *mihrab* on the inside.

Bab al-Nawfarah and Badreddin al-Hassan Street

The eastern gate of the mosque, Bab al-Nawfarah ('Gate of the Fountain') was originally part of the main *propylaeum* or monumental entrance to the inner *temenos* of the Roman temple, the climax of an approach which began from the *agora* further to the east and culminated in a huge portico (no longer surviving) and triple gateway (the present Bab al-Nawfarah). A broad flight of stairs descends from this impressive gateway, down into

Bareddin al-Hassan Street. At the bottom of the steps, on the right, is the *Al Naufarah* and opposite it the *Al Sham*, both lively places to stop for refreshments and watch the comings and goings along this street (see Cafés, page 55).

Continuing east along this street, after a little over 100 m you reach the remains of the **Triple Gateway**, which marked the eastern entrance to the outer compound of the Temple of Jupiter. The remains lie half buried in the ground, reducing their effect somewhat, though when you realize that the lintels which you can see just above ground level in fact crown the side portals, you get a sense of the original scale of the gateway. Like the monumental gateway at the end of Hamidiyeh Souq, the decoration is on the east-facing side.

If you follow the narrow street leading north immediately before the triple gateway (coming from the Umayyad Mosque), you can see on your left traces of the columns which formed the portico running around the outer courtyard of the Temple of Jupiter; in places just the column bases survive, elsewhere entire columns have been incorporated into the structures of buildings lining this street.

Continuing east from the triple gateway, the street becomes Qaimariyeh Street. Further along on the right is the **Al-Fatiyyeh Mosque**, built in 1742 as a *madrassa* by Fat'hy Effendi, a poet and Ottoman treasury official. This beautifully proportioned mosque is interesting for its combination of a typically Syrian/Mamluk style in the bands of black and white stone and the elegant decorative tiling, with a typically Ottoman plan in features such as the triple-domed porch that precedes the prayer hall. The overall effect, with a two-storey arcade around the quiet, shady central courtyard, is very pleasing.

Further east, Qaimariyeh Street gives way to a maze of narrow alleys extending northeast and southeast; following these alleys northeast gives access (with a little careful navigation) to the Christian quarter of Bab Touma.

Directly to the south of the Umayyad Mosque is the **Azem Palace**, which now also houses the Museum of Popular Tradition. To reach it, follow the narrow alley running south from the southwest corner of the mosque (this is **Souq al-Silah**, today largely given over to gold and jewellery, but previously the weapons market, or Souq Assagah), and turn left at what is effectively a T-junction.

Azem Palace and Museum of Popular Tradition

ⓘ *Wed-Mon 0900-1730 in summer, 0900-1530 in winter, closed Fri 1200-1430, S£150, students S£15.*

Built in 1749-1752 as a royal residence by the Ottoman governor of Damascus, Assad Pasha al-Azem, this palace is the largest, and amongst the most impressive, of the Ottoman period palaces to be found around Damascus. Entering it you are drawn immediately into another world of lavishly decorated rooms facing onto beautifully shady and tranquil courtyards with pools and fountains. The palace stands on the site of an earlier palace built by the Mamluk governor, Tengiz. It has been substantially restored, most notably after a fire in 1925, but the work was carried out carefully, preserving most of its original features. For a time it served to house the French Institute before being returned to the Azem family following independence. It was then sold to the Syrian government in 1951.

From the ticket booth, turn to the left and then right to enter the main *haremlek* or private family area. This, the largest courtyard, is particularly beautiful with its two pools and fountains, and its beds of tall, shady trees and shrubs. The rooms around the courtyard, luxuriously decorated with wood-panelled walls and ceilings, each contain displays along a different theme: musical instruments; a reception room with elaborate inlaid furniture; a marriage room containing beautiful glassware; a pilgrimage room complete with a richly embroidered *mahmal* (the camel-mounted palanquin used to carry dignitaries on the *Hajj* to Mecca); an armoury (daggers, swords, pistols and rifles); a 'grand' reception room; and the 'Salle de Djebel al-Arab', which houses various period costumes. There is also a private hammam complex and, in the south wall, a large, deep *iwan*.

A passage to the right of the ticket booth leads past carved wooden chests and panels and huge, richly decorated metal plates, through to the *salemlek* or visitors' area. There is another courtyard with a central pool which is surrounded by rooms, this time with displays more in line with a 'popular tradition' theme: domestic activities such as weaving and bread baking and handicrafts such as wood and metalwork, leatherwork, pottery, carpets, women's costumes and embroidered fabrics (some of them particularly delicate and beautiful).

Souq Bazuriye
The area extending west from the Azem Palace, between Hamidiyeh Souq and Mahdat Pasha Street, is well worth exploring for its souqs, khans and other historical monuments. Leaving the Azem Palace and turning left (south) into what is the main spice market, Souq Bazuriye, you pass on the left the **Hammam Nur ud-Din**, built by Nur ud-Din between 1154 and 1172 in order to raise funds for the building of the Madrassa al-Nuriyeh (see below). It is one of the oldest in Damascus and despite undergoing several restorations, and housing a soap factory for a time, it is today the best example of a fully functional Turkish bath complex in Damascus (see page 58). The large and elaborate domed reception chamber dates from the Ottoman period.

A little further along on the same side is the entrance to **Khan Assad Pasha** ① *Sat-Thu 0900-1500, S£75, students S£5*, built by Assad Pasha al-Azem between 1751 and 1753.

An imposing gateway of black and white stone leads through into what is easily the most ambitious and spectacular of Damascus's khans. It follows an essentially Persian design, with the main courtyard covered. There are a total of eight domes arranged around a large circular opening in the ceiling which allows light to pour down onto a circular pool below. Four huge pillars connected by elegant arches support the ceiling. Around the sides of the courtyard are two storeys of rooms (those below being the store rooms while those above were sleeping quarters). Above them there is a gallery running all the way round the walls, framed in arches which connect also with the arches of the four central columns to form part of the support for the eight domes. The alternating grey and white stonework, together with the ingenious and beautifully proportioned design of the building, combine to create something of an architectural masterpiece. Stepping into this khan from the crowded souq outside, you are overwhelmed by the scale and sense of space.

Following the street running due west from the entrance to the Azem Palace, you pass on the left the **Al-Azem Ecole**. Originally this was the Madrassa Abdullah al-Azem Pasha, built in 1770 by the man of the same name who later went on to become the governor of

Damascus and who represented the last of the Azem family, which governed Damascus between 1725 and 1809. Today the building houses an upmarket tourist souvenir/ antiques shop. Even if you are not interested in buying anything, the interior of the building is well worth a look, with its small courtyard and delicate columns and arches supporting a two-storey arcade around the sides. If you can get someone to take you up onto the roof, there are good views from here of the Umayyad Mosque.

Other madrassas and khans
Just past the Al-Azem Ecole there is a crossroads. Turning left into the narrow north-south street (**Souq Khayyatin**, the tailors' souq), immediately on the right is the entrance to the **Madrassa al-Nuriyeh**. Today the Mausoleum of Nur ud-Din is the only surviving part of this *madrassa*, which was built between 1167 and 1172 to house the tomb of one of the great Arab leaders of this period; two more modern mosques now stand on either side of the main courtyard. The mausoleum (which has itself undergone a certain amount of modification) is reached through a doorway on the left in the initial entrance hall. The mausoleum is kept locked but the caretaker is usually on hand to open it up. If not, you can peer in through the iron-grille window in the street, to the left of the main entrance. The simple chamber is topped by a tall honeycombed dome, with a band of Arabic inscription running around the walls and the marble tomb in the centre of the floor.

Continuing south along this street, on the right is the **Khan al-Khayyatin**, with a particularly beautiful arched entrance of alternating black and yellow stone with intricately carved decoration and Arabic inscriptions (though unfortunately partially obscured by small stalls on either side). Inside, the central dome has long ago collapsed although the arches which supported it still survive. The khan is occupied today by cotton embroidery and fabric shops.

Returning to the crossroads by the Al-Azem Ecole and Madrassa al-Nuriyeh, and heading north this time along the continuation of Souq Khayyatin, you pass first on the right the **Khan al-Harir**, the silk khan, the main entrance to which is via a narrow street on the right. The entrance doorway itself is the main feature of interest, being beautifully decorated. Continuing north, on the left is the entrance to the **Khan al-Jumruk** (the customs khan), a long L-shaped khan today occupied by brightly lit fabric shops, but still retaining its original domed roofing supported by arches.

If you head west from the crossroads by the Al-Azem Ecole and Madrassa al-Nuriyeh, following the main street, the second turning on the right (after about 200 m) brings you to the entrance of the **Maristan Nur ud-Din**. This can also be reached by taking a short detour from Souq Hamidiyeh (to do this, take the right turn at the point where there is a break in the corrugated-iron roofing of the Souq as you head east towards the Umayyad Mosque).

Maristan Nur ud-Din (or Bimaristan al-Nuri)

ⓘ *Sat-Thu 0900-1400, S£75, students S£5.*
Built by Nur ud-Din Zangai in 1154 as a hospital and medical school, this remarkable building was the most advanced medical institution of its time, and continued to function as a hospital until the 19th century. An archway with a honeycombed semi-dome frames the doorway, which utilizes a length of carved stone of clearly Roman/Classical origin as its lintel. The doors themselves, plated with metal and decorated with rivets arranged in

patterns, are original. The entrance hall has an impressive central honeycombed dome and semi-domes to either side, decorated with a mixture of honeycombing and stalactites. A band of Arabic inscription runs around the room just below the level of the main dome.

Inside the main courtyard there is a large central pool and fountain. In each of the four walls there is a deep *iwan*, and on either side of each *iwan* is a door leading through to a room containing exhibits of the **Museum of Arab Science and Medicine**, which is housed here. Note the beautiful arches of carved stone lattice work above each door.

Displayed in the rooms is a varied collection of items from the world of Arab medicine; bottles of medicinal herbs, pharmaceutical accessories for measuring, grinding, distilling, etc, surgical instruments for dentistry and operations, talismans and other 'spiritual medicine' accessories and also various astronomical instruments.

Arab medicine was far more advanced than anything practised in Europe during this period, and Western medical knowledge only really began to progress with the translation of Arabic texts into Latin. The Arabs, for example, were the first to develop alcohol-based anaesthetics that could be inhaled. A sponge was soaked in a potent solution containing amongst other things hashish, opium and belladonna. It was then dried and stored; only needing to be soaked in alcohol prior to use. Unfortunately the explanation boards here are only in Arabic and French, but the displays are fascinating anyway.

Straight Street

Known at its western end by its Arabic name, Madhat Pasha Street, the famous Via Recta, or Straight Street, runs through the entire Old City, terminating at its eastern end with Bab Sharqi. Along its length, and as short diversions off it, there are several important historical monuments.

The Via Recta originates from Greek times when, following the conquests of Alexander the Great, a grid pattern was imposed on the Old City, which at that time was centred on a low mound just to the south of the street. During the first century AD, the Romans widened the street to make it into a major axis through the city (the *Decumanus maximus*), a function that it continues to fulfil today.

In Roman times the street was around 26 m wide and lined with a colonnade, but over the centuries shops and buildings gradually encroached from either side, and today it is only a fraction of its former width. In fact at its western end, the tiny narrow souqs which run parallel to it just to the south were originally part of the same street, only becoming separated from it when shops and stalls were erected in the middle of the wide thoroughfare. The gate at this important entrance to the Old City, the Arab period **Bab al-Jabiye** (Gate of the Water Trough), standing on the site of the Roman Gate of Jupiter, is also in amongst these narrow souqs, although you can't see much of it today.

The first section of Madhat Pasha Street is a lively, bustling souq boasting a wide variety of shops and traders. On the left after around 300 m (shortly before the left turning into Souq Khayyatin) are the entrances to three khans. The middle one, **Khan al-Zait** (the Olive Khan), is quiet and unassuming but its overall effect is very pretty with its pleasant, shaded courtyard and central pool surrounded by two galleries of arched arcading.

A little further along on the right, just past the turning for Souq Khayyatin, is **Khan Suleiman Pasha**, a rather vibrant but dilapidated place, full of the lively disorder of functioning workshops. It was built for the Ottoman governor of Damascus, Suleiman Pasha al-Azem in 1732. An unimposing entrance takes you into a vaulted passage which leads through into a large rectangular courtyard. This was once covered by two large domes, now collapsed, although parts of the arches that originally supported them still survive. An upstairs gallery which can be reached via a staircase from the entrance passage runs around the whole courtyard.

Continuing east, after the next crossroads (left into Souq Buzuriye, right down towards Bab as-Saghir) the very much local-orientated shops and stalls of Mahdat Pasha Street start to give way to more touristy shops selling brassware, swords and inlaid woodwork. If you take the second right turn after the crossroads, by a square black and white stone minaret (a small sign marks the turning), after 100 m you reach the entrance of **Beit Nizam** ① *Sat-Thu 0900-1400, no admission charge*, on the left. This beautiful 18th-century Ottoman house once served as the British consul's residence in Damascus. Today it is once again in the hands of the Nizam family, but it is open to the public. The decoration around the walls of the innermost courtyard is particularly beautiful. Although the rooms themselves are not usually opened up for tourists, their interior decoration is truly lavish and you can at least peer in through the windows.

Returning to Straight Street, the first left turn after the turning for Beit Nizem brings you to the entrance of **Dar Anbar** ① *Sat-Thu 0900-1400 in summer, 0900-1300 in winter, no admission charge*, on the right, another beautiful old house built for a wealthy Ottoman merchant in 1867. The building was used as a secondary school from 1920 and currently houses the offices of a team of architects charged with the restoration and preservation of Damascus' historical monuments. The inner courtyard (*haremlek*) has been completely restored, and the decoration around the walls of the courtyard is particularly beautiful and delicate.

Continuing east along Straight Street, the next feature of interest is the remains of a **Roman Arch**, today contained within a garden to the right of the modern road. The triple arch was discovered by builders during the period of French rule, buried underground by centuries' worth of debris, and re-erected on the surface. It is thought to have formed part of a *tetrapylon*, which would have stood at what was once an intersection of the east-west *decumanus maximus* (Straight Street) with a major north-south street or *cardo maximus*.

If you take the right turn immediately before the arch, and then turn right again at the crossroads just after a small dog-leg in the street, you arrive at **Dahdah Palace** ① *Mon-Sat 1000-1300 and 1630-1800, ring the bell for entry, no admission charge*, on the left. This little detour is fairly well signposted, which is a good thing because from the outside this beautiful 18th-century house is entirely unremarkable. Inside, however, you have a typically Syrian/Ottoman layout of rooms arranged around a large, shady courtyard. The large, beautifully decorated *iwan* is particularly impressive.

The Roman Arch also roughly marks the start of the **Christian quarter**, which extends to the northeast, reaching up to Bab Touma. Just beyond the arch, on the left, is the Greek Orthodox Patriarchate, **St Mary's Church** (Al-Mariam). Looking somewhat modern, having been clad in bright new stone, this church dates back to 1867. Its predecessor was burnt down during the great massacre of Christians and Druze in 1860. The site has been occupied by a church since Byzantine times.

Continuing east along Straight Street, you arrive eventually at **Bab Sharqi** (literally 'Eastern Gate'). This is the only gate to preserve its original Roman plan (in Roman times it was the Gate of the Sun), but it has undergone extensive restoration, and only the left-hand arch of the triple arch (as viewed from the inside) contains any original stonework. Two columns stand just inside the gate, remainders of the colonnade that would have lined the street on either side during Roman times.

Christian Quarter churches

If you follow the narrow street to the left immediately before Bab Sharqi, at the end of this street is **St Ananias Chapel** ⓘ *daily 0900-1900, S£25*. A set of steps leads down to the cool, underground chapel reputedly standing on the site of the house of Ananias where Saul of Tarsus (later to become Paul the Apostle) was cured of his blindness. The chapel appears to have existed since Byzantine times, when it was known as the Church of the Holy Cross ('Musallabah' in Arabic).

Excavations first carried out on this spot in the 1920s revealed the apse of a small Byzantine chapel and, below it, the remains of a Roman temple. According to one line of reasoning, the house of Ananias was revered by early Christians. The Roman authorities, however, responded by building their own temple on the spot as a way of preventing Christians from coming here to worship. Only with the advent of the Byzantine era were the Christians able to build a church here.

St Paul's Chapel is popularly recognized as the site where Saul was lowered from the city walls to escape persecution by the Jews. It is reached by passing through Bab Sharqi and following the line of the city walls on the outside. The main road that you must walk along is particularly busy and unpleasant, but you have the chance to get a good look at this section of the Old City walls. The first stretch, as you walk from Bab Sharqi, consists mostly of recent restoration but as you approach Bab Kisan you can see the huge old Roman-period stone blocks in the lower courses, along with smaller stones from the Arab period higher up.

The chapel dedicated to St Paul is of 20th-century origin and, like the rest of the complex, belongs to the Greek Orthodox church. At the rear of the chapel you can see massive stone blocks, which are clearly of Roman origin. Originally the Roman gate of Saturn stood on this spot, but this was obliterated during the time of Nur ud-Din and the present gate into which St Paul's Chapel is built is a 14th-century Mamluk construction. The gate itself is best viewed from outside the walls. An arch frames the central door and above it is a single machicolation. On either side are towers with a band of carved decoration and medallions bearing the *Chi-Rho* symbol (adopted by Constantine as the symbol of the new Christian empire).

Northern gates and walls of the Old City

The city walls follow the same basic outline established in Hellenistic and Roman times, with a few minor variations. Various traces of the original Roman stonework can still be seen, although most of the surviving fabric of the walls is of Arab origin, dating from the 11th century onwards, when extensive repairs were carried out in order to strengthen the city's defences against the threat of Crusader and later Mongol attack. The gates of the Old City also generally correspond with the original Roman gates, although most have likewise been rebuilt in Arab times (Bab Sharqi, dealt with above, is an exception).

Bab al-Faraj (Gate of Deliverance), located in the northern city walls, close to the northeast corner of the Citadel, is one of the few gates which does not correspond with an earlier Roman gate. A gate was first built here by Nur ud-Din in the mid-12th century, although the existing double gateway is the result of later restoration. The inner doorway is a 13th-century Ayyubid reconstruction while the outer doorway is a 15th-century Mamluk reconstruction. In between the two, the covered passage between the two houses is a souq given over to blacksmiths and ironmongers.

Pass through the inner doorway and then, instead of turning left to go through the outer doorway, continue straight ahead (east) along Beit Nassorain Street, just inside the city walls. This picturesque, narrow lane is typical of the residential quarters of the Old City, with the ancient wood and plaster houses on either side leaning precariously and in one place actually touching, while elsewhere there are sections that are vaulted.

After around 250 m you reach a staggered crossroads. In front of you is the Saida Ruqqiyeh Mosque (see page 37), while turning left brings you to **Bab al-Faradis** (Gate of the Orchards, also known as Bab al-Amara and corresponding with the Roman Gate of Mercury). This gate is a 12th-century Ayyubid construction, and, like Bab al-Faraj, originally consisted of two parts, although today only the outer doorway along with a solitary arch of the inner doorway survives.

Continuing east from here, after another 250 m you reach **Bab as-Salaam** (Gate of Peace, corresponding with the Roman Gate of the Moon). This is the best preserved and most impressive of the Old City's gates. In its present form, the gate is once again a largely Ayyubid restoration dating from 1243, although an earlier reconstruction of the Roman original was carried out in 1172. The central arch contains within it a rectangular doorway topped by a massive lintel bearing an Arabic inscription, dedicated to the Ayyubid ruler Sultan al-Salih Ismael. On either side of the arch are large machicolations.

Pass through the gate to continue east (Bab as-Salaam is unusual in this respect in that it has an east-west alignment). For the first stretch the **Old City walls**, now to your right, are obscured by houses. But after a while the street crosses a stream (a branch of the Barada River) and runs between it and the city walls, giving you the chance to inspect them close-up. The large Roman stone blocks in the lower courses are clearly distinguishable from the smaller stones of the Arab and Turkish periods. In one place there is a column section which has been placed horizontally in the walls so that just its end is visible. The use of a Classical column to reinforce the structure of a wall in this way was a technique typical of the Crusaders, and was perhaps borrowed by the Arabs during 11th-12th century repairs to the walls.

At the end of the street you come out at **Bab Touma** (St Thomas' Gate, corresponding with the Roman Gate of Venus). Today this gate looks somewhat forlorn and dislocated, standing at the centre of a large, busy roundabout, the walls to either side having been dismantled to make way for the flow of traffic. The original Roman gate was reconstructed in 1227 during the Ayyubid period, with the Mamluk ruler Tengiz adding the machicolation in 1334. The gate takes its name from the son-in-law of the Byzantine Emperor Heraclius, Thomas, who led the resistance to the first Muslim assault on Damascus in AD 635. The gate gives its name to the Christian area that surrounds it, both inside and outside the walls of the Old City. The main thoroughfare running south from Bab Touma through this Christian part of the Old City intersects with Straight Street.

Beyond the Old City

There are a number of places of interest in the immediate vicinity of the Old City. People staying in the backpacker hotels of Souq Sarouja will be familiar with the picturesque old houses and narrow streets of **Sarouja district**. Less well known, however, is the extension of Souq Sarouja Street to the east of the modern Thawra Bridge.

Following this street east from Thawra Bridge, after about 500 m there is the **Towba Mosque** on the right (see Old City map). This large mosque was formerly a khan. According to local tradition, the khan gained a reputation as a brothel before being converted to a mosque – hence the name, which translates literally as Mosque of Repentance. The side entrance to the mosque (just off Souq Sarouja Street) is framed within a honeycombed arch, with a lintel bearing an Arabic inscription above the doorway. The courtyard, with its black and white stone paving, is reminiscent of that of the Umayyad Mosque, particularly in terms of the façade of the prayer hall. Inside the prayer hall, the *mihrab* is particularly beautifully decorated.

If you turn right at the junction by which this mosque is situated, and then right again immediately after, this narrow lane winds its way down to Al-Malek Feisal Street (if you go straight across the junction here you arrive at Bab al-Faraj). A short distance east along Al-Malek Feisal Street, on the right, is **Al-Mowalak Mosque**, also often referred to as the Bardabak Mosque after the prince, Bardabak al-Jaqni, who was responsible for its construction. The mosque has a beautifully decorated minaret in marble, along with an impressive honeycombed arch to the right of the main entrance.

Heading back west to Ath Thawra Street and then following it south, past the entrance to Souq Hamidiyeh, on the right after around 250 m is the **Darwish Pasha Mosque**. Built in 1574 by a governor of Damascus of the same name, the long façade of this mosque with its alternating bands of black and cream stonework is quite impressive, despite the pollution from the heavy traffic running past, which has left it in desperate need of cleaning. Inside, the pleasant courtyard with its central pool and fountain provides a peaceful respite from the frenetic activity outside. The panels of blue-glazed Damascene tiles on the façade of the prayer hall are particularly beautiful. Inside the prayer hall there is more tiling and an attractive *mihrab*, although a massive, intruding chandelier spoils the overall effect somewhat. The small octagonal building attached to the mosque by an arch contains the tomb of Darwish Pasha.

Continuing south, just past the entrance to Madhat Pasha/Straight Street, on the left this time, is the **Sinan Pasha Mosque**. The mosque dates from 1590, during the reign of an Ottoman governor of Damascus, Sinan Pasha (not to be confused with the great Ottoman architect of the same name who was responsible for the Tekkiyeh as-Suleimaniyeh mosque; see below). The façade is in the alternating black and cream bands of stone typical of Mamluk and Ottoman architecture, while the minaret is clad in distinctive green and turquoise glazed stone. Inside, there is once again a peaceful, shady courtyard and more panels of beautiful Damascene tiling in the arcades around the courtyard.

Just south of the Sinan Pasha Mosque, the road forks. Bearing right to head in a southerly direction, you are on Qasr al-Hajjaj Street, which becomes Midan Street a bit further south. Although now somewhat swamped by modern development, this axis represents the once distinct **Midan Quarter**, which extended south for several kilometres. Its significance lay in the fact that this was the route taken by pilgrims as they set off from the Old City on the *Hajj*, or pilgrimage to Mecca. As such, it developed over the centuries into an important thoroughfare lined by numerous mosques, mausoleums, religious schools, baths and other amenities catering for the pilgrims. The monuments strung out along this route are today in a somewhat dilapidated condition, and only for the really dedicated sightseer.

Bearing left at the junction just south of the Sinan Pasha Mosque to follow the line of the Old City walls, you pass through **Souq Sinaniye** with its stores selling sheepskins. Bearing left at the next fork, you are in Badawi Street, which heads east, passing on the left the **Bab as-Saghir** gate to the Old City (literally 'Little Gate', corresponding with the Roman Gate of Mars). The large stone blocks of the Roman foundations can still be seen, though the rest of the gate is a combination of Nur ud-Din's 12th-century reconstruction and later Ayyubid work.

To the southeast is the Muslim **Bab as-Saghir Cemetery**, an important place of pilgrimage for Shi'ites who come to visit two of the tombs there. One is the **Tomb of Fatima**, daughter of the Prophet and wife of Ali. The other is the **Tomb of Sukeina**, the daughter of Hussein and great-granddaughter of the Prophet. Most scholars agree that these are unlikely to be the genuine tombs of these two figures, but the tradition persists, attracting large numbers of Shi'ites from Iran. To enter, follow Al-Jarrah Street, which branches southwest off Badawi Street and runs through the centre of the cemetery; a gate on the left gives access to the southern half of the cemetery containing the two tombs.

Modern Damascus

In many ways, modern Damascus is just like any other large capital city the world over, with it congestion, pollution and faceless high-rise developments. At the same time, however, it does manage to retain a certain Syrian feel to it in places. This is particularly true of the area round Martyrs' Square, where the hawkers, market stalls and hole-in-the-wall restaurants, selling roasted half-chickens and *falafel* or *shawarma* sandwiches, leave you in no doubt that this is an Arab capital. Heading for the commercial districts around Yousef al-Azmeh Square, the bland uniformity of airline offices, expensive hotels and shops selling fancy designer goods starts to assert itself more strongly. By the time you get out to the districts such as Abou Roumaneh, where the foreign embassies have made their home amidst affluent, fashionable residential areas, there is little to remind you that this is not Europe or America.

There is no doubt that the Old City and its environs are the main focus of historical interest in Damascus, but the modern city has its important monuments and places of interest too. The most notable of these are the Tekkiyeh as-Suleimaniyeh complex and the National Museum, next to each other on the south bank of the Barada River, just to the south of the busy east-west thoroughfare of Shoukri al-Kouwatli Street.

Tekkiyeh as-Suleimaniyeh Complex
ⓘ *The mosque itself is fenced off and closed to the public for important restructuring and restoration work at the moment, but you can see its beautiful façade and peaceful grounds from the alleyway.*
This large complex includes a mosque (currently closed to the public) and a *madrassa* (religious school), which now houses a handicrafts market. The mosque was built by

Sinan Pasha, the great Ottoman architect (most famous for the Suleimaniye Mosque in Istanbul), in honour of the Sultan Suleiman I (Suleiman the Magnificent, 1520-1566). Its purpose was to provide an alternative starting point for the annual pilgrimage to Mecca, the organization of which was traditionally the responsibility of the governor of Damascus.

From the arched entrance off Omar Ben Abi Rabeea Street, a pedestrian lane lined with jewellery and antique shops leads to the main mosque. Halfway down on the left is the entrance to the old **Madrassa as-Selimiyeh**. This was actually a later addition, built during the reign of Suleiman's successor, Sultan Selim II (1566-1574) by another architect. The courtyard, with its subsided and uneven floor of black and white stone slabs and central fountain and pool, is rather atmospheric, with a slightly dilapidated charm about it. The surrounding arcade of arches and small domed rooms would once have housed religious students but is now given over to various handicrafts: inlaid woodwork, brass, copper and silverware, embroidered fabrics, paintings, carpets, musical instruments, etc.

The **Tekkiyeh as-Suleimaniyeh Mosque**, although not particularly grand in terms of its size, is a wonderful gem of Ottoman architecture. The mosque itself is clearly Turkish in inspiration, with its domed prayer hall and pointed, rocket-like minarets rising up on either side. The doorway of the prayer hall is decorated with honeycombing and delicately carved stalactites, while inside there is beautiful glazed blue and white tiling in the arches above the windows and doors. The courtyard in front of the mosque is more typically Syrian in design, with its black and white stone slabs and large central pool and fountain. Surrounding it on three sides are rooms originally meant to house the pilgrims preparing for the *Hajj*.

National Museum

ⓘ *Shoukri al-Kouwatli St, Wed-Mon 0900-1800 in summer, 0900-1600 in winter, S£150, students S£10, café and toilets are located within the museum grounds, no photography allowed.*

The National Museum of Damascus is the largest in Syria and boasts a wealth of artefacts covering some 11 millennia of Syria's rich history. Many of the great historical and archaeological sites in Syria, despite their importance and often spectacular settings, are stripped of their most important artefacts, and it is here that you have the opportunity actually to see them. Your appreciation of the vast majestic site of Dura Europos, for example, will be greatly enhanced if you can remember the fabulously preserved murals of the Jewish synagogue, or the Valley of the Tombs in Palmyra by the reconstruction of the Yarhai Hypogeum, both housed here. Likewise, it is the artefacts of sites such as Mari and Ebla that actually hold the key to appreciating their significance. Indeed, given the size of the collection, it is perhaps worth making two visits in order to appreciate this museum fully, ideally at the beginning and end of your trip.

The gardens of the museum contain numerous architectural fragments and items of statuary, often overlooked by visitors but well worth wandering round. The massive entrance to the museum consists of a reconstruction of the façade of the Umayyad Palace of Qasr al-Heir al-Gharbi in the Syrian desert to the west of Palmyra, which was dismantled and transported here piece by piece.

To your right as you enter is the long west wing of the museum, containing the **pre-Classical** and **Arab-Islamic** collections, grouped for the most part according to the site (eg Ugarit, Ebla, Mari, etc). In the two upper floors of this wing there is a permanent exhibition of **contemporary art** (mostly paintings and some sculpture) as well as a rather desultory **prehistoric** section. To your left as you enter is the east wing, containing **Classical** and **Byzantine** collections. (So, if you want to view the exhibits chronologically, you have to go back and forth between the two wings.)

For those with a specialist interest, the excellent though outdated *Concise Guide* (which is anything but concise) is usually on sale at the ticket office (though it periodically sells out and the process of ordering another print run is painfully slow). Alternatively, if there is an organized group receiving a guided tour it is worth tagging along. Otherwise it is really a case of exploring and discovering as best you can for yourself.

The labelling throughout the museum has got a lot better in the last few years and detailed plaques are popping up all over the museum. There is also a massive futuristic overhaul of the museum planned for some time in the near future. It is not possible to give a detailed commentary on such a formidable a collection here, but there are certain collections/reconstructions that do deserve a special mention.

Probably the most famous aspect of the museum is the reconstruction of the mid-third century AD **Dura Europos Synagogue** at the far end of the east wing, across a small courtyard. Discovered at the site of Dura Europos in the 1930s, the synagogue is unique in that its walls were decorated with frescoes depicting scenes from the Old Testament, including human representations – something which goes against all Talmudic traditions. Equally remarkable is the fact that these frescoes should be so well preserved (because they were buried under sand). The walls of the synagogue consist of the original frescoes, much faded by time but still extremely impressive. The ceiling is a reconstruction of the original, with its painted wooden beams. It is unlit and receives little natural light (in order to protect the frescoes) so it takes a while for your eyes to adjust to the gloom.

Immediately before the courtyard leading to the synagogue, a flight of stairs leads down to the early second-century **Hypogeum of Yarhai** from the Valley of the Tombs in Palmyra. The hypogeum (underground burial chamber) is reconstructed from the original, giving an excellent insight into what these underground tombs would have originally looked like, with the compartment-shelves for sarcophagi built into the walls and sealed by funerary busts, while at the end of the main chamber to the right is the *triclinium*, where a funeral banquet would have been held.

Returning to ground level, stairs also lead up from here to the first floor and the **Salle de Hommes**. This contains an impressive collection of jewellery and coins, including iron and gold funerary masks discovered near Homs and dating from the first century AD.

Hejaz railway station

Completed in 1917, the Hejaz railway station marks the terminus of the famous railway line that ran from Damascus to Medina. The brain-child of the Ottoman Sultan Abdul Hamid II (1876-1909), the main purpose of the railway was to facilitate the passage of pilgrims undertaking the *Hajj* to Mecca. However, with the outbreak of the First World War, it became a vital transport and communications link for the Ottoman and German forces, leading to concerted attempts by the Allies to blow it up.

The interior of the building is worth inspecting, with its beautifully decorated wooden ceiling and balcony running around the main hall, and its large silver chandelier. Outside there is a steam engine on display, dating from 1908. No train services leave from the Hejaz station anymore.

Historical Museum of Damascus

ⓘ *The entrance to the musuem is set back from Ath Thawra Street just to the north of Thawra Bridge, via an arched gateway in the parking area of a government building Sat-Thu 0800-1400, S£75, students S£5.*

Little visited by tourists, this museum occupies the large **Beit Khalid al-Azem** (the palace of a former prime minister, Khalid al-Azem). The extensive complex is divided into a northern section which houses the museum, and a southern section which houses an important archive of historical documents not officially open to the public. From the entrance on the north side of the palace, a small initial courtyard leads through to the main courtyard, dotted with trees and shrubs, and with a fountain and pool on one side. This was the private family area of the palace (the *haramlek*). A large *iwan* occupies part of one wall, while the various rooms around the courtyard contain the museum's exhibits.

The quality of the decoration in the rooms is superb, easily matching that of the more famous Azem Palace in the Old City. Lavishly carved marble-work and intricately decorated wood panelling adorn the walls and ceilings and there are numerous items of inlaid wood furniture. One room contains an intriguing fountain, fashioned from stone into something that resembles a water-maze, which was used for games. Another room contains large scale models of the Old City, Salihiye district and various buildings and complexes around Damascus, as well as an interesting collection of old photographs.

A doorway at the end of the passage to the left of the *iwan* leads through to the southern half of the complex. This represents the public visitors' areas (the *salemlek*) and consists of a series of three courtyards. This is where the archive is housed and, although it is not officially open to the public, it is often possible to wander through and admire the impressive exterior decoration of the courtyards and rooms. If you do make it through to here, you can exit via the south door which leads out onto the eastern extension of Souq Sarouja Street.

Salihiye/Al Charkasiye district

Most of the monuments in this district are concentrated along Madares Assad ud-Din Lane. Generally closed to the public, you can admire their façades from outside. The lane is lively and atmospheric; full of vegetable stalls by day and shops serving *fuul* and hummus at outside tables by night. The approach to this district, northwest of the city centre, is through areas dominated by modern development. However, as you reach the lower, gentle slopes of Mount Kassioun, the streets begin to get narrower and the layout less regular.

This area was first settled during the mid-12th century when Hanbalite refugees, fleeing in the wake of the Crusader occupation of Jerusalem, were housed here by Nur ud-Din, who was keen to keep them separate from the rival Shaffi school that was predominant within the walled city. It then began to absorb the overspill from the walled city and with time became a well regarded district in its own right, inspiring many members of the ruling class to build mausoleums, mosques and *madrassas* in the area.

Mohi ud-Din Mosque

Roughly halfway along Mardares Assad ud-Din Lane, this mosque is open to the public and has a particularly beautiful Mamluk-style octagonal minaret. The mosque dates from the early 16th century and was built over the 13th century burial chamber of the famous Sufi mystic, Mohi ud-Din Ibn al-Arabi. It remains an important pilgrimage site for Sufis. Inside, to your left as you face the prayer hall, a flight of steps leads down to a domed chamber decorated with glazed blue and white tiles which houses the tomb of Al-Arabi. His tomb is the largest, contained within a silver grill surrounded by glass. The four other tombs in the chamber are of two of his sons (the double-tomb); Sheikh Muhammad Kharbutli, a devoted follower of Al-Arabi; Mahmoud Pasha Sirri al-Khunaji, a son-in-law of an Egyptian Khedive; and Abd al-Kader al-Jazairi, a famous Algerian patriot who resisted the French occupation of his country before finally being exiled to Damascus.

Hanbala Mosque
To the east of Mohi ud-Din Mosque, in a side street north off Madares Assad ud-Din Lane, this mosque dates from the early 13th century and was founded by Sheikh Omar Muhammad al-Maqdisi, the leader of the Hanbalite refugees from Jerusalem. Enclosed within unassuming (and easily missed) walls, the mosque interestingly has six classical columns in its courtyard.

Mount Kassioun

ⓘ *There is no public transport to the summit; unless you have your own transport, you must take a taxi, in which case you are advised to negotiate a return trip since there is little traffic along this road.*

Rising steeply to the northwest of Damascus is Mount Kassioun (1200 m), a bare, dry ridge of mountain which dominates the city on this side and provides a useful point of orientation. The mountain has a number of legends attached to it. A mosque built over a cave on the eastern slopes of the mountain, near the town of Barzeh (on the road to Saidnaya) is believed to mark the birthplace of Abraham. Most famously, it was from the summit of Mount Kassioun that Muhammad is said to have looked down on Damascus, not daring to enter this oasis of gardens and streams lest its earthly delights distracted him from his quest for heavenly paradise.

There are several good vantage points on its lower slopes that can be reached via the narrow lanes leading off to the north from Madares Assad ud-Din Street in Salihiye district. But the best views out over Damascus are from the top, reached via a road which hairpins its way up the mountain. In summer there are various cafés and stalls close to the summit where tourists and Damascenes alike come to enjoy the cooler air and take in the panorama of the city spread out below: today a sprawling urban mass which is a far cry from the paradise of greenery said to have so impressed Muhammad, but nevertheless an impressive sight. The best times to come up here are late afternoon for sunset over the city, and at night when it is lit up in all its glory.

Saida Zeinab Mosque

ⓘ *A taxi to the mosque will cost around S£200-300 one way, depending on your bargaining powers. To get there by microbus (servees), take one from Fakhri al-Baroudi St to 'Garagat al-Sitt' (in the southern suburbs of Damascus), and change there for Saida Zeinab Mosque (Jamiaat Saida Zeinab). Non-Muslims are not allowed inside the prayer hall but you can get a good view from the courtyard outside. Women must wear the provided abeyya, men should not wear shorts or short-sleeves.*

This fascinating mosque 10 km to the south of central Damascus, like the Saida Ruqqiyeh Mosque in the Old City, is an important place of pilgrimage for Shi'ite Muslims. It is also similar to its counterpart in the Old City in that it is relatively modern, Iranian-built and equally bright and colourful in its decoration. The huge square courtyard features towering circular minarets in two corners and a large gold-domed prayer hall in the centre. Practically every wall surface, including the entire height of the minarets, is decorated with boldly coloured glazed tiles bearing riotous floral patterns or elegant Qur'anic calligraphy. The overall effect is very striking. Inside the prayer hall, the decoration is even more exuberant, with patterned mirror-work complementing the coloured glazed tile-work. In the centre of the prayer hall is the **tomb of Saida Zeinab**, the granddaughter of Muhammad (there is another mosque of the same name in Cairo which also lays claim to being the burial place of Saida Zeinab). The tomb is protected by a silver grille and is almost invariably surrounded by crowds of pilgrims seeking her blessings or intervention.

Damascus listings

For Sleeping and Eating price codes and other
relevant information, see pages 8-10.

🛏 Sleeping

Damascus *p20, maps p21, p28 and p30*
Damascus has a distinct lack of decently priced
mid-range and budget accommodation. In
part, this is due to many hotels in these
categories catering solely for the busy Iranian
pilgrim market, which books up entire hotels
years in advance. Most of the hotels below
cater mainly to the foreign tourist market so
you'll only be battling other tourists over a bed
rather than a busload of Iranians. Especially in
summer, it's best to book ahead (at least for
your 1st night) in Damascus. Conversely, those
after luxury accommodation are now spoilt for
choice in the city. In recent years a whole host
of new boutique hotels, set in fabulously
restored old palaces, have opened up in the
Old City. If you want to treat yourself, then this
is the city to do it.

Most of the mid-range and budget
accommodation is based in the New City
with the budget hotels strung out around
the leafy alleyways of Souq Sarouja and in
neighbouring Martyr's Sq. Be aware that
Martyr's Sq is the red-light district of
Damascus and many of the budget hotels
(not the ones listed below) in this area
double as brothels.

$$$$ Antique Khan, off Ameen St, Old City,
T011-541 9450, www.antiquekhan-hotel.com.
Tucked away down a tiny alleyway, the
Antique Khan has unusual rooms (some on 2
levels) all with a/c and satellite TV. There's a
shady leafy courtyard, lots of local artwork on
display and cheerful staff.
$$$$ Beit al-Mamlouka, opposite
Hammam Bakri, just off Bakri St, near Bab
Touma, Old City, T011-543 0445,
www.almamlouka.com. An exceedingly
special boutique hotel festooned with lamps,

traditional textiles and antiques. Attention to
detail is key here and not a penny has been
spared in preserving the building's character;
from the gorgeous floor tiling and gloriously
restored original hand-painted ceilings in
some of the rooms to the fact that all the
mod-cons (a/c, satellite TV) are not on show.
A wonderfully atmospheric place to stay.
$$$$ Beit Rumman, Bab Touma, Old City,
T011-545 1092, www.beitrumman.com. It's
the super-friendly service here that sets this
little hotel apart. In a wonderful 300-year-old
house with opulent tile-floors and old
stonework, the staff here work hard to
provide the personal touch. Rooms are all
individually decorated and come with a/c,
satellite TV and Wi-Fi. There's shady seating
areas in the internal courtyard, a basement
bar exclusively for guests' use and a rooftop
terrace with views over the city.
Recommended.
$$$$ Oriental, Abbara St, near Bab Sharqi,
Old City, T011-543 5336, www.orientalhotel-
sy.com. The subtle, yet elegant rooms here
have lovely old carpets and antique brass and
silverware on display. All surround a peaceful,
plant-filled shady courtyard that's the perfect
respite after a day sightseeing. Rooms have all
the usual mod-cons (a/c, satellite TV and
Wi-Fi), and the utterly charming staff are
happy to help fulfil your every wish.
$$$$ Talisman, Tal el-Hajara St, Old City,
T011-541 5379, www.talismanhotels.com.
Despite the dramatic red internal walls that
are a touch more Moroccan *riad* than
Damascene house, this old Jewish palace is a
heavenly dream. The whole place oozes
film-star glamour with rooms (a/c, satellite TV,
Wi-Fi) lavishly furnished with antique in-laid
furniture and chandeliers, and a small
swimming pool on-site.
$$$ Afamia, Furat St, T011-222 8963,
www.afamiahotel.com. Beloved by tour

groups, the Afamia is a solid choice in a central location, with exceptionally friendly and helpful staff. Some of the older rooms are a little kooky (ask to see a few before deciding) but they're all spotlessly clean and come with a/c, satellite TV and Wi-Fi.

$$$ French Palace, 29 May St, T011-231 4015. Popular with local tourists, the grandma- style rooms here are all chintz and frills and come with a/c and satellite TV. It's a clean, well-maintained hotel and although there isn't much English spoken, the staff are welcoming.

$$$ Orient Palace, Hejaz Sq, T011-222 0502, www.orientpalacehotel.net. This grand old relic has seen better days, but if you can get past the obvious need for an interior update you can focus on its bygone era charm. Rooms (a/c, satellite TV, fridge) are sparsely furnished but beds are made with crisp white linen and the front rooms have balconies with excellent views over Hejaz Sq.

$$$ Salam, Ibn Sina St, T011-221 6674, salamhotel@mail2world.com. Hidden away down a quiet alley behind the Hejaz Railway Station, this hotel has clean, decent-sized rooms (a/c and satellite TV) that are comfortably furnished if a little bland.

$$$ Sultan, Al-Baroudi St, T011-222 5768, sultan.hotel@mail.sy. This long-standing travellers' haunt has helpful management and a cheerful communal lounge. Unfortunately the bright, clean rooms here (a/c and fan), are much too basic for the price. See if you can bargain them down.

$$ Al-Haramain, Bahsa St, Souq Sarouja, T011-231 9489, alharamain_hotel@ yahoo.com. You can't go wrong with this Damascus backpacker institution that has spick-and-span clean rooms (fan only) with incredibly high old-style beds that all share clean bathrooms. It's in an atmospheric 800-year-old building with lovely old tiling on the floors and a small leafy courtyard to hang in. The staff here are friendly souls and can help with any query. Recommended.

$$ Al-Rabie, Bahsa St, Souq Sarouja, T011-231 8374, alrabiehotel@hotmail.com. Just up the road from the Al-Haramain, the Al-Rabie has a wide variety of simple clean rooms (fan and fridge, some with a/c, shared bath), and a couple with attached bath. There's a huge courtyard always abuzz with fellow travellers, a roof-top dormitory for the budget-conscious, and management are helpful and efficient.

$$ Al-Saada, Souq Sarouja St, T011-231 1722. This quiet little hotel has basic rooms (fan only, a couple have attached baths) surrounding a shady courtyard that is covered in vines.

$$ Ghazal, Souq Sarouja St, T011-231 3736, www.ghazalhotel.com. The friendly Ghazal is a funky little place run by brothers: Muhammad, Ahmed and Said. There's a wide variety of clean, simple rooms (with fan, some with attached bath), a kitchen guests can use, and a large communal area decked out with traditional touches.

$ Al-Amin Al-Jadid, Straight St, Old City, T011-542 0297, alaminhotel@yahoo.com. The friendly Al-Amin Al-Jadid is a welcome addition to the cheap hotel scene and the only budget accommodation option in the Old City. The rooms (fan only) are as basic as they get but the owner is a kind-hearted soul, there's free tea on offer at any time of the day, and the shared baths are kept clean. Recommended.

Long-stay accommodation

If you're planning on studying Arabic for a few months in Damascus (or staying in the city a long time for other reasons) it's more economic to rent a room than stay at the budget hotels. The shops along Bab Touma in the Old City usually display flyers in their windows advertising rooms for rent around the city and the 2 places below specialize in renting rooms to students of Arabic.

Damascus Hostel, Alkeshleh al-Abbara St, Old City, T011-541 4115, www.damascus

hostel.com. This ramshackle, cheerful place has very simple rooms (fan only) that share baths, a kitchen, and groovy communal areas. There's free tea, coffee and water and a really friendly, homely, atmosphere. You can also stay here for shorter terms (though it's quite expensive if you're not staying for a whole month).

House of Damascus, behind Azem Palace, Old City, T0944-318 068, www.houseof damascus.com. Just like staying in your own share-house. This peaceful old house in the middle of the Old City has rooms with satellite TV and fan that share 2 baths. There's a small courtyard and shady terrace and 2 well-equipped little kitchens to use, making it perfect for long-stayers. Booking is essential.

🍴 Eating

Damascus p20, maps p21, p28 and p30
Damascus is the place to splash out and treat yourself in a swanky restaurant. Many of the best restaurants are based in the Old City and are set in beautifully restored old houses that ooze atmosphere. Even better, a meal in these restaurants won't break the bank. There's generally a 10% government tax added to your bill at all the fancier places.

For cheap eats, the city is awash with little fast-food places. In the New City, Martyr's Sq has loads of *shawarma* and juice stands, all along 29 May St there are bakeries churning out Syrian pizza and on Hejaz Sq there's a bustling fast-food joint that serves good burgers, *shawarma*, chips and all manner of greasy goodness to late at night.

In the Old City there are 2 cheap and cheerful *shawarma* and *falafel* stalls basically opposite each other on Badreddin al-Hassan St. Both have seating on the pavement and the one on the left (walking towards the Umayyad Mosque) does a decent Syrian-style burger as well. There are bakeries and juice stands galore dotted around the Old City.

††† **Old Town**, near Roman arch, just off Straight St, Old City, T011-542 8088. Daily

1300-1700 and 1930-late. This long-established place has a lovely courtyard (covered in winter) as well as indoor seating. The rather posh clientele come for the Italian and French dishes (including fresh pasta) but Arabic specialities are served as well. There's a pianist most evenings and alcohol is served.

†† **Al-Kamal**, 29 May St, 1100-late. This old-timer restaurant in the New City has been around for years and still has a loyal following for its French-inspired dishes and friendly service.

†† **Al-Khawali**, Straight St, Old City, T011- 222 5808. Daily 1200-0200. Once you've had a meal here you'll soon see why so many famous faces (President Bashar al- Assad and King Carlos of Spain among them) come to Al-Khawali when in Damascus. Set in a wonderful old Damascene house, with tables in the huge courtyard or upstairs, this place has superb service, and an extensive menu with its own original takes on Syrian specialities as well as French- inspired dishes. Don't forget to order the *Al-Khawali hummus*; it's to die for.

†† **Casablanca**, Hanania St, Old City, T011-541 7598. Daily 1230-0100. An upmarket, elegant place set in a beautifully restored old building. The food is primarily French with Arabic touches and there's live music in the evenings.

†† **Leila's**, Umayyad mosque east-side, Old City. Daily 1100-late. Come here to eat on the rooftop terrace, with its gorgeous views over to the Umayyad mosque. The menu is a good mix of Arabic and continental and the salads are particularly good. The service can be a little sloppy and check your bill when paying as they've a habit of overcharging. Alcohol available sometimes.

† **Al-Masri**, Said al-Jabri St (sign in Arabic only). Closed in the evening. More closely resembling a narrow corridor than a restaurant, this clean, simple and unpretentious place is popular with locals for lunch and often busy. They serve a wide selection of Egyptian food (the restaurant's name is 'The Egyptian') at very reasonable prices and have a menu in English. The *fatteh* dishes are extremely generous and filling, Also a good place for *fuul* lovers to come for breakfast.

♈ Art Café, Tal el-Hajara St, Old City. Daily 1200-late. This cosy stone-walled restaurant does pasta, pizza and *falafel* plates all at reasonable prices. The staff are friendly and you can come here just for a coffee or beer.

♈ Bakdach, Souq Hamidiyeh, Old City. Daily 0900-late. Join the huge queue at this Damascene institution, all waiting for their serving of delicious local-style ice cream. It's the perfect antidote to a hot day in the city and each cone comes covered in a generous helping of crushed pistachios.

♈ Pizza Roma, just off Maisaloun St. Daily 1000- late. A small, clean diner-style place offering good-value pizzas, spaghetti and lasagne.

Cafés

Al-Naufarah, Badreddin al-Hassan St, Old City. Damascus' most famous café is at the bottom of the steps leading down from the east wall of the Umayyad Mosque. It's an extremely popular place to come and hang out for both Damascenes and visitors, and a great place to watch the general comings and goings or just rest after your sightseeing extravaganzas. In the evenings the café is host to the famous storytelling show of Abu Shadi (about 2000 daily) which, although in Arabic, is a captivating performance and the last of an ancient oral-storytelling tradition.

Al-Sham, Badredding al-Hassan St, Old City, Across the alley from the Al-Naufarah, the Al-Sham is another popular traditional café with pavement seating.

Dominos, Bab Touma, Old City. Daily 0930-late. This Parisian-style café and restaurant, dishes up great salads, crêpes and sandwiches, as well as making the best cappuccino in the city. The pavement terrace is always full of hip young things checking

each other out and it's a great refuel stop after a few hours of walking around the city.

Eco-Café, north-side of the citadel. This peaceful little place is set within a colourful riot of blooming flowers and greenery that is the bio-diversity and ecological gardens of Damascus. It's a wonderful idea and a great place to escape the city.

Souq Sarouja, Crnr Souq Sarouja St and Bahsa St. A popular, simple little place with tables that spill out across the roadside. In the evenings, pretty fairy lights twinkle and groups of friends come to puff on *narghile* and play backgammon.

✪ Entertainment

Damascus *p20, maps p21, p28 and p30*
Bars
There are plenty of little pubs in the Christian Quarter of the Old City, particularly by Bab Sharqi and along Bab Touma St. Of the restaurants and cafés above, you can just go for a drink at **Art Café** and **Dominos**.

Karnak, Martyr's Sq. Open 1100-late. For something a little different; this smoky little bolt-hole is up the stairs inside a liqueur store and has cheap big cans of local and imported beer, friendly service and brilliant views of the Martyr's Sq traffic chaos below. It's frequented mostly by solitary male drinkers who sit for hours puffing on *narghile* and drinking whiskey, but they're used to tourists dropping in.

Ninar Art Café, off Bab Sharqi, Old City. Daily 1000-late. This stone-walled place on 2 levels is a popular choice with locals and tourists alike. It's got a slightly bohemian vibe and there's decent pizza if you're feeling peckish. There's a decently stocked bar and big bottles of beer are served in blissfully chilled glasses.

Piano Bar, off Bab Sharqi (towards St Ananias Chapel), Old City. Daily 1200-late. If you love bad singing then karaoke at the Piano Bar makes for a highly entertaining night out. If you don't, it's best to stay away. Food is served as well.

Cinema

Cham Cinema, inside Cham Palace Hotel, Maisaloun St. There's a mixed-bag of Hollywood blockbusters, local movies and European art-house films on show at this small theatre.

Cinema City, inside Cattan Hotel building, Barada St. This modern cinema shows the latest Hollywood blockbusters as well as Middle Eastern movies.

Traditional shows

Abu al-Azz, just off Souq Hamadiyeh, signposted 'al-Azz Al Shamieh hall'. Daily 0900-late. The narrow passageway entrance, where delicious savoury pastries are served, conceals a spacious restaurant upstairs on 2 floors, elaborately decorated with marble mosaic walls and painted wood ceilings. All day long there's live Arabic music to listen to while you eat and at about 2200 every evening diners here are entertained by a Whirling Dervish performance.

✪ Festivals and events

Damascus *p20, maps p21, p28 and p30*
Jul/Aug Jazz Lives In Syria Festival, 1 week of international jazz performances held at Damascus citadel.

Sep Silk Road Festival, a program of cultural events celebrating this ancient trade route with events held in Damascus, Aleppo and Palmyra.

Nov Damascus Film Festival, a celebration of independent film-making, showcasing many new pan-Arab productions at venues across the city.

◯ Shopping

Damascus *p20, maps p21, p28 and p30*
Damascus is a shopper's paradise with myriad selection of souvenirs to choose from. There are antiques, brassware, ceramics, woodwork, textiles and jewellery galore as well as cheap spices for the foodies, original paintings for the art hunter, all manner of swords for the military buffs and not forgetting the brocades and silks that Damascus is so justly famous for. The Old City is the obvious place to start looking and a rough guide to the shopping districts contained within it is below. The New City has a large handicrafts market set in the grounds of the Madrassa as-Selimiyeh (see page 47), where many artisans display their products. At nearly all places it's the norm to bargain.

Abu Jawal, just off Straight St, Abu Jawal's tiny shop is full of beautiful hand-painted blue and white tiles and ceramics that he makes himself. He's a friendly soul and you can watch him work as you browse.

Anat, Bab Sharqi. A beautifully presented store that sells high-quality, gorgeous textiles; made by women in the Palestinian refugee camp and women's cooperatives all over Syria. The women all share in any sales profits. There are lovely bags, bedcovers, shawls and cushion covers in dozens of colours and designs. It's a wonderful project and well worth your support.

Aram, Straight St, just before the Roman Arch. This place has a huge range of colourful etched and hand-painted glass from dainty tea-glasses to wine goblets and everything in between. There's a fascinating array of colours and designs from traditional Arabic to verging on the contemporary.

Balah Shoes, Qaimariyeh St. Hundreds of different styles of traditional leather sandals and moccasin-style shoes. If you can't find the style/size you want, Mr Balah (who is deaf but lip-reads in English) can custom-make a pair especially for you.

Shahin Art, just off Straight St, www.mshahinart.com. Writer and artist Mahmoud Shahin has built up quite a cult-following among travellers to Syria. He started painting seriously 15 years ago as a way of expressing his thoughts on religion and philosophy, after his novels were banned from being published. Since then he's held exhibitions in Europe as well as Syria. His tiny art gallery is filled to the brim with his modern and quirky original pieces.

Tekkiyeh as-Suleimaniyeh Handicrafts Market, Madrassa as-Selimiyeh, off Omar Ben Abi Rabeea. Along a pleasant shady alley strung with vines, 1 block over from the National Museum, a whole host of jewellers and craft stalls have been set up. Half-way down the alleyway is the entrance to the Madrassa as-Selimiyeh, which was once a school of religion but now houses artisan's workshops. There's original artwork, textiles and hand-painted furniture as well as leatherwork, ceramics and in-laid woodwork on offer. It's a good place to get an idea of what's available and an easy hassle-free place to browse and shop.

Old City shopping guide

Souq Hamidiyeh is the most famous shopping street in the Old City and a great place to stroll along, although much of what's on offer is aimed at local shoppers. There's brilliant browsing potential with meringue wedding dresses and lots of rather raunchy underwear on show. There are also lots of traditional clothing stalls, brocade, leatherwork, *narghile* stores and a few antique places here.

Around the **Umayyad Mosque** are numerous tourist-orientated shops. Around the plaza at the western entrance (as you come out of Souq Hamidiyeh) there are some high-quality stores selling jewellery, lamps, ceramics and inlaid wooden boxes. Following the walls of the mosque around to the southern and eastern sides is a whole host of tiny stalls selling a wide range of gifts (a lot of it cheap and cheerful tat).

Souq al-Silah running off the southern side of the Umayyad Mosque is all glittering with gold. Follow the road straight along until it turns into **Souq Bazuriye** (just after Azem Palace) and the gold is replaced with spice, natural remedies, perfumes and natural oils, and sweets.

Straight Street (Madhat Pasha St) has a kaleidoscope of shopping opportunities. At the Bab al-Jabiye end it's devoted to clothing with lots of *galabeyya* and *kuffiyeh* (the traditional chequered head-dress) shops. Then the spice and nut stalls begin to dominate, but the further up the road you walk (towards Bab Sharqi) the more antique shops begin to appear. You can hunt through brassware, silverware, brocade, woodwork and textiles, as well as glassware, ceramics and furniture.

Badreddin al-Hassan and Qamariyeh St runs off the eastern end of the Umayyad Mosque and there's original artwork, antiques, jewellery, clothing, textiles and woodwork to browse through.

Bookshops

There are a number of ad-hoc news-stands where you can find foreign newspapers, and a good news-stand on Straight St between the Roman Arch and Bab Touma St, though it only seems to be open in the mornings. Titles on offer include the *Herald Tribune*, the *Guardian*, the *Daily Telegraph* and the *Times*, as well as magazines such as *Newsweek*.

Avicenne, Al-Tuhami St. On a little street running parallel to Maisaloun St, this bookshop has a good selection of English- and French-language books on Syrian, Arab and Muslim history, art and architecture as well as some second-hand novels.

▲ **Activities and tours**

Damascus *p20, maps p21, p28 and p30*
Arabic language classes
Damascus is a centre for Arabic language studies, and institutes offer courses on all levels of study from beginner to advanced. There are also many private tutors offering lessons (usually from S£300-1000 per hr).
Arabic Language Centre, Damascus University, Mezzeh Highway, T011-212 9494, www.arabicindamascus.edu.sy. The ALC has an excellent reputation and is a popular

choice among foreign students of the language. They run 12-week courses throughout the year for all levels of study. Classes generally run from 0900-1300, 5 days per week and cost approximately US$300 per course plus an initial placement test fee of S£500.

Arabic Language Institute, Mezzeh, Villat Sharkiyya, T011-613 2646, arabicinstitute@ mail.sy. There are 6 different levels of Arabic available with 14-week long courses starting on 1 Feb, 1 Jun and 1 Oct. Course fees are approximately US$200 per course, with an initial placement test fee of S£200. Classes run 5 days per week from 0900-1230.

Hammams

Hammam Bakri, Bakri St, T011-542 6606. Sat-Thu, women 1000-1700, men 1700-2400. Popular with tourists, this well-run place offers sauna, massage and scrub for about S£400.

Hammam Nur ud-Din, Souq Bazuriye, T011-222 9513, men only. Daily 0900-2400. This beautiful old building is the most famous hammam in the city as well as one of the oldest. The full works here is about S£600.

Hammam Silsila, north side of Umayyad Mosque, T011-222 0279. Men only, daily 0900-2300. More basic than the Nur ud-Din, you can opt just for a sauna here or for the full scrub treatment.

Hammam Ward, off Souq Sarouja St. Women Tue-Wed 1200-1700, men daily 0700-2400 (except Tue-Wed women's hours). For a total local experience head to this dilapidated building that's over 800 years old. They hardly ever see tourists and you'll get a hearty welcome. There are definately no frills and no English is spoken but you'll be scrubbed raw and squeaky clean at the end. Sauna and scrub costs approx S£400.

Tour operators

Most of the mid-range hotels and all of the luxury hotel can arrange guides, and cars with driver, and the Tourist Information Centres should be able to provide a list of qualified city guides for you. Some of the budget hotels can arrange day trips to places like Krak des Chevaliers. There are dozens of tour companies in the city all churning out the same-style tours.

Beroia Travel and Tourism, Bab Sharqi, Old City, T0933-221138, www.beroiatravel.com. Run by the dynamic May Mamarbachi, this excellent travel company specialize in doing off-beat, specialist-interest tours that cover Damascus, Syria and neighbouring countries. There are cooking tours, architectural tours, trekking and camping trips and day tours of old Damascene houses and little known Damascus art galleries. They focus on the personal touch here and certainly deliver. May can help you tailor-make a program to suit your needs and wants. 3 times a year (in May, Sep and Oct) they run fabulous cooking tours (that take in the historical sites as well) with chef, Anissa Helou. Recommended.

Eco-tourism Syria, www.ecotourismsyria.com. A young travel company that focus on nature projects as well as historical sites, going to places off the main tourist trail such as Al- Jabbul wetlands and Al-Talila nature reserve. The company aim to support bio-diversity projects and conservation within Syria.

Transport

Damascus *p20, maps p21, p28 and p30*
Air
Damascus International Airport, T011-453 0201 (flight enquiries T167), is 25 km to the southeast of the city centre and is Syria's main hub for international flights. A taxi from the city centre costs approximately S£700 but be prepared to pay more than this late at night. The airport bus unfortunately only runs from Mezzeh, not into the centre of town, so isn't practical for getting there. The airport has a branch of **CBS** bank for foreign exchange and ATM, car rental firm offices, a hotel

reservations desk, a tourist information office, and an extremely cheap duty-free shop.

Most of the airline offices are based on Said al-Jabri St, around Hejaz Sq, including **Syrian Air**, T011-168 (for central reservations) and T011-169 (airport), or opposite the Cham Palace on Maisaloun St.

Domestic Distances between towns in Syria are generally small enough that you don't need to fly. If you do decide to take a domestic flight, **Syrian Air** has 2-3 flights daily to **Aleppo** (1 hr, S£1742); 2-3 flights daily (except on Tue) to **Lattakia** (1 hr, S£1242); 5 flights per week to **Qamishle** (1½ hrs, S£2242); and 2 per week to **Deir ez-Zor** (1½ hrs, S£1992).

International Syrian Air operate direct international flights to **Amsterdam**, **Athens**, **Cairo**, **Dubai**, **Istanbul**, **London**, **Madrid**, **Munich**, **Rome** and **Vienna**, among others. Other carriers that fly out of Damascus include **BMI** (T011-223 9800), **Emirates** (T011-231 3452), **Egypt Air** (T011-223 3093), **Gulf Air** (T011-221 1267), **Royal Jordanian** (T011-221 1267), and **Turkish Airlines** (T011-222 7266). International airport departure tax is S£1500 but this is currently being phased out (and added into the cost of your flight). Ask your hotel for up-to-date information.

Bus

Damascus has 2 main bus stations: Harasta Pullman Station for all destinations north of the city and Al-Samariyeh Station for the south. Both stations are out of town. A taxi to either from the centre costs about S£90 and takes about 25 mins (except in peak traffic, from about 1600-1800, when you should give yourself 1 hr to get there). Services are generally frequent enough that you can just turn up at the station and be on your way within an hour. You have to show your passport when buying bus tickets.

Harasta Pullman Station (Garaget Harasta Pullman): There are at least 30 companies here providing transport to all destinations to the north of Damascus, mostly on a/c buses. **Kadmous** and **Al-Ahliah** are 2 of the most reliable companies to use. **Kadmous** has several departures daily to **Aleppo** (4½ hrs, S£200), via **Hama** (3 hrs, S£115) at 0700, 1010, 1230, 1400, 1600 and 1900; **Raqqa** (6 hrs, S£225), via **Homs** (2½ hrs, S£115), at 1200, 1315, 1430, 1600, 1730 and 2300; **Deir ez-Zor** (7 hrs, S£300), via **Palmyra** (3½ hrs, S£175) at 0615, 0930, 1130, 1330, 1430, 1600, 1730, 1930 and 2230; and **Qamishle** (9 hrs, S£350) via **Hassakeh** (8 hrs, S£325) at 1230 and 2300. They also have buses to **Tartus** (3 hrs, S£200), every hour from 0530 and **Lattakia** (4 hrs, S£225), every 2 hrs from 0530.

International International services from the Harasta Pullman station: there are also a couple of companies offering transport to **Istanbul** but you'll always have to change buses in Antakya (just over the border). It's always cheaper to go to **Antakya** direct from Aleppo.

Al-Samariyeh Bus Station (Garaget Al-Samariyeh): The huge, dusty Al-Samariyeh Bus Station can be slightly disconcerting at first glance but it's actually easy to navigate. It consists of 3 different car parks. The first (where some lazy taxi drivers drop you off) is full of microbuses. Walk to the back-left exit of this car park and you reach the Pullman Bus Station. Beyond this car park is the International Service Taxi car park. In the Pullman Station, there are about 6 companies that head to towns south of Damascus, as well as international services to **Amman** (Jordan) and **Beirut** (Lebanon). The companies also have a habit of swapping routes between each other but if you turn up to one ticket booth and they are no longer plying that route, they will point you in the right direction for the company that is.

At the time of writing **Al-Rashed** were the only company with services to **Bosra** (1½ hrs, S£100). Buses start at 0800 and leave every 2 hrs until 2000. **Damas Tour** run buses to **Suweida** (1½ hrs, S£70), and **Shahba** (1½ hrs, S£70). Buses start at 0600 and run every hr until 1900. **Al-Muhib** have services to **Deraa** which leave every 30 mins from 0800 (1½ hrs, S£80).

International services from the Al-Samariyeh bus station: There are a couple of different companies offering international services but **Challenge** seem to have the best buses. They have 2 normal services to **Amman** in Jordan, at 0830 and 1430 (5 hrs, S£500) and 1 VIP service at 1730 (S£700). To **Beirut** they have 1 bus per day which leaves at 1500 (4 hrs, S£400).

In the car park behind the Pullman station here are **international service taxis**. They tend to be a quicker (and more comfortable) option than the bus because you don't have to wait for an entire bus-load to fill out border procedures. Taxis leave at all times of the day, when full. A seat to either **Amman** or **Beirut** costs S£700.

Car hire

Budget (www.budget-sy.com) have 3 offices in Damascus: Argentina St (T011-224 4403) 29 May St (T011-231 8116) and at Damascus International Airport (T011-540 0070). **Europcar** (www.europcar-middleeast.com) have several offices throughout the city. The most central being inside the Meridian Hotel on Shoukri al-Kouwatli St (T0988-777 664). **Marmou Car Hire** (www.marmou.com) is a good local car-hire company and have an office at Damascus International Airport (T011-333 5959).

Microbus

Microbuses are useful for getting to the smaller towns in the surrounding area that aren't serviced by the Pullman buses. There are 2 microbus garages that travellers will find useful. **Maaloula Garage**, to the south of Abbasseen Sq, has frequent microbuses leaving for **Maaloula** (1 hr, S£40), and **Saidnaya** (1 hr, S£30). From **Abbasseen Garage**, just to the east of Abbasseen Sq, you can get a microbus to **Nabak** (for **Deir Mar Musa**) (1 hr, S£30).

Train

Kadem Station handles all incoming and outgoing train services. It's outside the city centre; a taxi here costs about S£70. The fast trains to Aleppo are particularly good, and are well worth considering as an alternative option to the bus.

There are 3 express services to **Aleppo** (4¼ hrs, 1st class S£240, 2nd class S£200), via **Homs** (2¼ hrs, 1st class S£135, 2nd class S£110), and **Hama** (3 hrs, 1st class S£165, 2nd class S£165), at 0700, 1615 and 2015. There's also a slow train at 1500.

There's an old slow train daily to **Lattakia** (5 hrs, S£155) via **Tartus** (4 hrs, S£115), at 1515 and a train at 1815 every day to **Deir ez-Zor** (7 hrs, 1st class S£200, 2nd class S£135), via **Raqqa** (5 hrs, 1st class S£165, 2nd class S£110).

Services on the old diesel-fired steam train that used to ply the scenic route from Damascus to the Barada Gorge unfortunately no longer begin from Damascus. This may change in the future so enquire at the station for up-to-date information. If you're a train journey enthusiast and want to ride on this train, you now have to journey out to Al-Hamie Station (about S£300 in a taxi) where you can pick up the service which runs daily (during summer months) at 1025 to Ain Fijeh. The return service to Al-Hamie leaves Ain Fijeh at 1700. See page 68.

International The Hejaz rail service between Damascus and Amman is currently suspended. If services do resume (and track maintenance along this line has been going on an awfully long time now so there's no guarantee they will), please be aware that this train journey can be a painfully slow, dusty and uncomfortable process (taking an average 9 hrs); though there's no denying the atmospheric experience of travelling along this route. Before services were suspended, trains left Damascus (Kadem Station) on Sun at 0730 arriving in Amman at 1700 (S£200). Tickets could only be bought on the day of travel.

🅘 Directory

Damascus *p20, maps p21, p28 and p30*
Banks
Banks generally stay open later than the rest of the country in Damascus. Main branches (such as the **Commercial Bank of Syria – CBS** branches stated below) are generally open Sat-Thu 0830-2000 and Fri 0830-1400. Most banks in the city now have ATMs that are linked to the international networks. Be aware that cards on the maestro network don't work in some ATMs. In the New City, banks are clustered around Hejaz Sq and Yousef-al-Azmeh Sq, including branches of **CBS** which deal with foreign exchange and have ATMs. If your maestro card doesn't work in the **CBS** ATM, try the **Bank of Trade and Industry** ATM on Hejaz Sq. They generally work in this one. In the Old City there is a **Bank of Syria and Overseas** on Mouawela St that has an ATM that takes all foreign cards and an ATM opposite the **Maristan Nur ud-Din Museum** that is linked to the foreign networks.

Cultural centres
Take your passport with you if you want to be admitted to any of the centres. The **American Cultural Centre**, 87 Ata al-Ayoubi St, http://damascus.usembassy.gov/resources.html, is closed to the public until further notice (check the website for

up-to-date details on this). **British Council**, off Maisaloun St, T011-331 0631, www.britishcouncil.org/ syria, Sat-Thu 0900-2000, is geared mostly to providing English-language courses, though they organize the odd event. The library here has a limited collection of books, mostly focusing on Britain. Upstairs on the 3rd floor there is a cafeteria with a selection of British newspapers on offer. **Centre Culturel Français**, Bahsa, T011-231 6181, www.ccf-damas.org, Mon-Sat 0900-2100, by far the most active of the cultural centres in Damascus, is housed in a large modern building complete with its own theatre/cinema and exhibition hall. A programme of events, published every 3 months, is available from the centre listing the varied programme of films, theatre, music, exhibitions, etc they organize. **Goethe Institute**, 8 Adnan Malki St, T011-371 9435, www.goethe.de/INS/sy/dam/deindex.html, has a programme of events, published bi-monthly (in German), which lists films, lectures, music, exhibitions, etc.

Embassies and consulates
In an emergency citizens of New Zealand and Ireland should use the UK embassy and Australian citizens should use the Canadian embassy.

If your passport is lost or stolen, your embassy should be able to help you obtain a replacement. However, except in the case of extreme emergencies, most foreign embassies are very reluctant to do anything else for their nationals.

Belgium, Al-Salaam St, No 10 (2nd and 3rd floor), Mezzeh east, T011-612 2189, www.diplomatie.be/damascus. **Canada**, Lot 12, Mezzeh Highway, T011-611 6692, www.syria.gc.ca. **Egypt**, El-Galaa St, Abu Roumaneh, T011-333 2932. **France**, Ata al-Ayoubi St, Al-Afif BP 769, T011-339 0200, consulat@ambafrance-sy.org. **Germany**, Abdul Manen Al-Riad St, T011-332 3800, www.deutschebotschaft-damaskus.org. **Italy**, al-Ayoubi St, BP 2216, T011-333 2621, www.ambdamasco.esteri.it. **Japan**, 18 Al-Mihdi Bin Baraka St, Abu Roumaneh, T011-333 8273. **Jordan**, Mezze Eastern Villas, Western Tarablus St, Building 27, T011-613 6260. **Netherlands**, Al-Jalaa St, Im Tello, Abu Roumaneh, T011-333 6871. **Spain**, Shafi St, Mezzeh East, T011-613 2900. **Turkey**, 58 Ziad Bin Abi Sufian St, Abu Roumaneh, T011-333 1411. **UK**, Kotob Building, 11 Muhammad Kurd Ali St, Malki, T011-373 9241, www.britishembassy.gov.uk/syria. **USA**, 2 Al-Mansour St, Abu Roumaneh, T011-339 1444, www.usembassy.state.gov.

Internet

There are dozens of internet cafés dotted around the city. Some ask to see your passport to register and some don't. **Damascus Internet** is located inside the main post office on Said al-Jabri St. **Internet Zone** is just of Souq Sarouja St, conveniently placed for people staying in the budget hotels. In the Old City **Mission Net** has friendly service, super-fast connections and new computers and is on Straight St, while **Dot Net** is on Bab Touma St.

Medical services

You won't have any problems finding a pharmacy in Damascus, they're everywhere. There are some excellently stocked large pharmacies in the new town along Port Said St. Damascus has several good private hospitals with high standards of medical care. **Shami Hospital** Ibrahim Hanano St, by junction with Jawaher Lal Nahro St, T011-373 5094 has English-speaking doctors and also includes a dental clinic.

Post

The **Main Post Office** is on Said al-Jabri St, Sat-Thu 0800-1900, Fri 0900-1400. The **EMS** (Express Mail Service) office is around the corner. It's better to send parcels by EMS rather than by regular mail. **DHL** has a branch nearby, just off Omar Ben Abi Rabeea St, Sat-Thu 0800-2000, Fri 0900-1400.

Telephone

There are numerous **Easycomm** card-phones dotted all over Damascus, with phonecards on sale from nearby shops, kiosks, juice bars and the like; just ask around. Finding a card-phone may be no problem, but the challenge is to find one which is not right next to a hopelessly busy/noisy junction or main road.

Visa extensions and travel permits

For **visa extensions** head to the **Passport and Immigration Office** on Furat St, between Martyr's Sq and Said al-Jabri St, Thu-Sat 0800-1400. You need 3 passport photos, a letter from your hotel, and must return to collect your passport the next day. This is one of the busiest places to extend your visa, and as well as having to come back the next day, expect to have to wait around quite a bit. Moreover, according to many travellers, the staff here are none too friendly or helpful. If you can time it right, it is far better to get this done elsewhere in Syria. The office at Aleppo is fairly efficient (same-day service), or go for a smaller town such as Tartus, Hama or Lattakia. You should be able to get a 2-month visa extension here. For **Quneitra Permits** you have to go to the **Ministry of the Interior** just to the north of Adnan Malki Sq, in Salihiye, Sun-Thu 0800-1400. You will need your passport, details of your car registration number and (if you've hired a driver), his name and ID number. Permits are free and valid for same day or the next day but if you've hired a driver it's best to go on the same day so that you can show his ID number.

Around Damascus

Damascus is a convenient base from which to explore the surrounding countryside. The places covered here are all easy day trips (or less) from the capital. ➺ *For listings, see page 72.*

Damascus to Maaloula

From the Citadel, head north along Ath Thawra Street, over the flyover and under the underpass, following the signs for 'Barzeh'. Follow the road round to the right at *Ibn Nafis Hospital* (around 4 km from the centre of Damascus) and then go straight, ignoring the fork to the right soon after signposted for Aleppo and Lattakia. Just under 2 km beyond the *Ibn Nafis Hospital*, turn left at a crossroads. After this turning, there are frequent signs for Saidnaya and Maaloula. The road winds its way through rocky hills, passing first through the village of **Barzeh**, behind which, on the eastern slopes of Mount Kassioun, is a shrine said to mark the birthplace of Abraham. Around 4 km after the crossroads, bear right where the road forks (signposted), and then bear left soon after (not signposted). The road by now has emerged onto a wide flat plain. Around 27 km from Damascus you reach a large modern roundabout; go left here to ascend to the town of **Saidnaya.**

If you continue straight on past this roundabout, a little under 2 km further on there is a second roundabout with a newly built hospital beside it and a left turn signposted for Saidnaya. Around 600 m beyond this there is another left turn for Saidnaya, followed immediately after by a left turn leading up to **Cherubim Convent** (see page 67). Continuing straight along the main road, after around 15 km you pass through the large village of **Al Tawani**, before arriving at a T-junction (just under 24 km from the turning for Cherubim Convent). Turn left here (you pass soon after through a pair of concrete arches, complete with towers and crenulations, which mark the start of **Maaloula** village), and it is another 4 km into the centre (turning right takes you down to the main Damascus–Homs motorway). Arriving in the village, bear right at a roundabout, follow the road round to the right and then sharply left through an S-bend to climb up to Deir Mar Takla. Note that if you are heading for Saidnaya from Maaloula, the small right turn after you pass through the concrete arches is signposted only as an alternative route back to Damascus.

Maaloula → *For listings, see pages 72.*

Famous mostly for being one of the few places in Syria where Aramaic, the language of Christ, is still spoken, Maaloula is an important centre of Christianity. The town's butter-yellow and pale-blue houses are stacked higgledy-piggledy on top of another, huddled strikingly against the sheer cliffs that mark the edge of the Qallamoun mountains.

Some of the caves around Maaloula suggest that it was a centre for prehistoric settlement, while others appear to have been dug during Greek and Roman times and subsequently used by the early Christians as refuges from persecution. The occurrence of Aramaic in the region, together with the inscriptions found in some of the caves, confirm Maaloula as one of the earliest centres of Christianity in the world. Later, during the Byzantine period, Christianity flourished in the area.

Ins and outs

Getting there and away There are microbuses from Damascus and from Saidnaya to here. Most microbuses will drop you off at the top of the hill at the Convent of St Takla car park saving you a walk up hill. When leaving, they pick up down the hill at the main intersection.

Deir Mar Takla (Convent of St Takla)

According to legend, this convent grew up around the shrine of St Takla (or St Thecla), daughter of one of the Selucid princes and a pupil of St Paul. The legend relates how Takla was being pursued by soldiers sent by her father to execute her for her Christian faith. Finding herself trapped against the sheer cliffs of Qallamoun, she prayed to God for help. Her prayer was answered when a narrow cleft was opened in the rock face, allowing her to escape to a small cave high up in the cliffs. St Takla is recognized locally as the first Christian martyr, although quite how this is so, when according to the legend she escaped her pursuers and lived in the cave until her peaceful death, is not entirely clear.

Most of the buildings of the current convent are of recent origin, and none show any evidence of surviving Byzantine work. The main chapel has a number of icons inside, while the shrine of St Takla is above, in the side of the rock face.

The defile

From the parking area to the left of the convent, a path leads up through a narrow defile, the rock on either side pressing in, almost to form a tunnel in places. This is the cleft in the cliffs referred to in the legend of St Takla, and there are numerous shrines and caves which have been dug into the rock along its length. It is also to this defile that Maaloula owes its name, the word meaning literally 'entrance' in Aramaic. The defile brings you out eventually at the top of the cliffs. Close to where it emerges, there is a restaurant with a pleasant garden terrace set amongst poplar trees. Bear left and follow the road up past the *Safir Maaloula* hotel to reach the monastery of Mar Sarkis. If you do not wish to walk, you can get to the monastery by car – bear left at the roundabout in the village.

Deir Mar Sarkis

① *Daily 0800-sunset, no admission charge but donation appreciated, shoulders and knees to be covered on entering the church, no photography allowed.*

The monastery of St Sarkis (or St Serge, from Sergius) is believed to have been founded in the early fourth century AD, on the site of an earlier Greek/Roman temple dedicated to Apollo. St Sarkis, along with St Bacchus, to whom the monastery is dedicated, were soldiers in the Roman army based at Rasafeh. Having converted to Christianity, they refused to make sacrifices to the god Jupiter and were put to death. Their remains are believed to have been housed in the large basilica there, and during the Byzantine period Rasafeh was known as 'Sergiopolis' in honour of St Sarkis.

The entrance to Deir Mar Sarkis is through a low, awkward doorway, presumably a defensive feature. This leads through to a small, recently restored courtyard. On your left is a room labelled 'Museum and Souvenirs'. There is an excellent series of postcards of the monastery's icons on sale here, along with various items of religious kitsch. The square pit hewn out of the stone floor in this room was for pressing grapes.

At the far end of the courtyard, on the right, a passage leads through to the monastery's church. The main altar of the church, in the central apse, is of particular interest, consisting of a semi-circular slab of marble with a 7-cm rim around it. The fact that the altar is semi-circular is taken as evidence that it dates from before AD 325, the date of the First Council of Nicea, when it was decreed that all altars had to be flat and rectangular. The rim around the edge of the altar is thought to be a feature surviving from pagan times, when altars were used for animal sacrifices in which the blood had to be collected. As the monks of the monastery are quick to point out, however, the rim appears to have been simply a stylistic feature, as in this case there is no drainage point from which to collect the blood, nor is the rim engraved with the animals which were suitable for sacrifice, as was the norm on pagan altars. Below the altar is a small crypt. In the side-apse to the left is another altar, this one also with a rim, though rectangular in shape. Note the fresco in the dome above the altar, depicting the heavens with the Virgin Mary and Jesus surrounded by the saints Mathew, Mark, Luke and John.

The iconostasis of the church includes a number of particularly beautiful icons painted by St Michael of Crete in the early 19th century. The one above the entrance to the central apse is of St Sarkis and St Bacchus. On the pillar to the right of the entrance to the central apse is something you don't see often: Christ's crucifixion and the Last Supper portrayed in a single icon. It is also unusual in that Jesus is seated to the right of the table rather than in the centre. Also of interest is the icon of St John the Baptist, here smiling and relaxed, with his legs crossed (in contrast to the usual serious/formal depictions), having baptized Jesus and therefore completed his mission. Some of the icons in the church are thought to date back as far as the 13th century.

There is clear evidence in the church of its ancient origins. The lower part of the iconostasis consists of stone slabs taken from the earlier Greek/Roman temple, while some of the capitals appear to have originated from the same source. Above the arches separating the nave from the side aisles, wooden beams can be seen incorporated into the stonework. These are thought to have served to reinforce the church against earthquakes. Samples taken from them have indicated that they are Lebanese cedar, and around 2000 years old, suggesting that they too were recycled from the original temple. Outside the church, around the side, there is an even smaller arched entrance, now protected by a porch and sealed behind a metal door. In the immediate vicinity of the monastery there are several substantial rock-cut caves.

Maaloula to Yabroud

The road leading from the centre of Maaloula up to Deir Mar Sarkis is also the road to Yabroud. Some 4 km from the roundabout in Maaloula, turn right at a T-junction and then keep going straight, passing through two villages before descending steadily to reach the town of Yabroud, 19 km from Maaloula. En route, the Qallamoun mountains present a very different aspect, sloping up gently to the west, and revealing themselves as part of the plain itself, tilted up and sheared off to create the sheer cliffs that characterize the setting of Maaloula as seen from the east. Shortly before arriving in Yabroud, you pass on the right more rock-cut tombs dating from Roman times. Bear left as you enter the town to reach the centre; right takes you directly on to the Damascus–Homs motorway.

Yabroud

There is evidence of settlement in the area of Yabroud going back at least to the Mesolithic period (10,000-7500 BC), while in Roman times the town appears to have formed part of the territory placed under the control of Agrippa II. Its importance can be surmised from the discovery in Rome of an altar dedicated to *Malekiabrudis* or Jupiter Malek of Yabroud, the local form of Jupiter. Today Yabroud is a sizeable, prosperous and rapidly growing town, thriving on the narrow strip of fertile agricultural land in which it is set. In the centre there is the large Greek Catholic **Cathedral of Constantine and Helen**. This is thought to stand on the site of an earlier Temple of Jupiter, with stones from the temple having been incorporated into the fabric of the cathedral. Inside, the cathedral consists mostly of modern restoration, although there are some beautiful icons and traces of Roman architectural fragments in the apses. On the edges of the town the remains of another ancient church are being incorporated into a new church of modernistic design. Following the main road northeast out of Yabroud, after 8 km it joins the Damascus–Homs motorway just south of the town of Nabak. This route also offers a more interesting alternative for part of the otherwise motorway-bound journey between Damascus and Homs.

Saidnaya

Saidnaya's origins go back to ancient times, with evidence suggesting that it was inhabited at least from the sixth century BC, when it was known by the Aramaic name of 'Danaba'. Evidence of occupation can be found right the way through Greek and Roman times, and it emerged as an important centre of Christianity well before this became the official religion of the Roman Empire. By the time of the Crusades, Saidnaya was second only to Jerusalem as a centre of pilgrimage for Christians. Despite the town's impressive array of convents, monasteries, churches, chapels and shrines, today Saidnaya has a modern, nondescript air in places due to the plethora of new construction in the town.

Ins and outs
Getting there and away   There are microbuses from Damascus, Maaloula and Nabak to here. Microbuses from Maaloula tend not to be as frequent.

Sights
In the centre, perched on a rocky hillock overlooking the town is the Greek Orthodox **Convent of Our Lady of Saidnaya**. From a distance it looks for all the world like a fortress and some people argue that this was the function it originally served. The convent is an important pilgrimage site for Christians and Muslims alike, the object of veneration being an icon of the Virgin Mary supposedly painted by St Luke. According to legend, the convent was founded by the Byzantine Emperor Justinian during the sixth century. Much damaged by earthquakes and the passage of time, today the convent is a jumbled mixture of old features and new restoration, much of the latter undertaken in recent years. Flights of stairs zigzag up from the parking area below the convent to the small low doorway leading inside. (Alternatively the tower to the left houses a lift.)

The main chapel has numerous painted gold icons and a wooden *iconostasis* in front of the altar. The pilgrimage shrine, known as *Shaghoura* ('the famous') is a small dark room around the right-hand side of the chapel on the outside. The icon attributed to St Luke is kept hidden in an ornate silver-doored niche, while either side of this there are a number of later icons. Numerous beaten silver crosses and other religious symbols left by pilgrims are pinned to the walls. The large room off the courtyard to the right of the shrine houses a small museum, containing mostly painted gold icons. You will need to track down someone with the key if it is not open.

The hillock on which the convent is perched was certainly the site of earlier shrines, including possibly a sun temple dating from Greek and Roman times. As you ascend by the road up to the car park below the convent, a **cave tomb** is visible cut into the side of the rock, sealed by a metal door. Above it are three carved niches each containing a pair of figures (today very worn and headless) and a conch shell semi-dome in the arch of the niches. Greek inscriptions date these tombs to AD 178, although in all probability they were first inhabited far earlier. Around Saidnaya there are a number of caves which have shown evidence of settlement since the early Stone Age, the most important of these being in the low rocky mound by the roundabout as you approach Saidnaya.

Amongst the houses that cluster around the convent there are numerous other small churches, monasteries and shrines dedicated to various saints. Some are very old, although the majority of these have undergone extensive restoration. The **Church of St Peter**, situated by the roundabout below the Convent of Our Lady of Saidnaya, on the southeast side, is a remarkably intact Roman building that has remained almost completely unmodified since its conversion to a church.

Just over 2 km to the northwest of Saidnaya, and accessible only by foot, is the **Monastery of Mar Thomas**, also originally a Roman Temple which was later converted into a monastery. The route is not obvious, so walk in the general direction and then ask – you should be pointed along the correct track with a bit of luck. The main building is a squat structure set in a courtyard. It has been partially restored, with a new cross of white stone now standing on the top. The building is locked and the keys kept at the main convent.

Around 8 km to the northeast of Saidnaya, strategically situated on the highest point of the local Qallamoun mountain range, is the **Cherubim Convent**. From the turning off the main Saidnaya–Maaloula road (see above), the narrow road winds its way steeply up to the convent, offering some excellent views along the way. The church itself is a small building, restored in 1982 when a new roof was added, but incorporating three classical columns and some huge stone blocks which attest to its origins sometime during the third century AD.

Today the church is dwarfed by a large and somewhat ungainly new school/orphanage. The keys to the church are held by the resident caretaker. Dotted around the grounds are various architectural fragments from Greek and Roman times. Adjacent to the church is a rocky outcrop topped by two crosses, from where there are panoramic views out over the town of Saidnaya and the surrounding countryside.

The Barada Gorge to Zabadani and Bloudan

From Damascus you can follow the narrow Barada river up through low hills which mark the southwest extremities of the Anti-Lebanon range, eventually arriving on the wide fertile plain of Zabadani. The town of Zabadani is the largest of several hill resorts in the area and popular amongst Syrians as a weekend retreat from the stifling summer heat of Damascus. The scenic route via the 'old' Zabadani road runs up through the green and well-wooded Barada gorge and is well worth the trip if you have your own car. This is also the route taken by the old narrow-gauge railway which, at the time of research, was still running from Al-Hamie to Ain Fijeh (before Zabadani) during the summer months. Services along this line are by an ancient Swiss-built diesel-fired steam train which hauls equally antiquated wooden carriages. It's an excruciatingly slow trip and the main reason for taking it is for the scenery and the novelty value (see page 60).

Damascus to Zabadani via the old road
From Umawiyeen Square head west along the continuation of Shoukri al-Kouwatli Street, keeping the Sheraton hotel on your left (signposted 'Dumar'). Continue straight through the busy town of Dumar (or 'Douma'). Around 10 km from Umawiyeen Square, shortly after passing the Barada Beer brewery on the left, there is a fork in the road with a petrol station in the wedge of the fork. Bear right here and just under 1 km further on you arrive at a T-junction with a large dual-carriageway. Go left here and right immediately after to rejoin the old Zabadani road.

The road first descends into a valley, the floor of which is surprisingly green and well-wooded, before starting to climb steadily, passing through several villages.
There are various summer restaurants along the road as it winds its way through the Barada gorge. Although their setting amongst shady trees is pleasant enough, the river itself – generally little more than a stream – is unfortunately very polluted, particularly in summer when most people visit and flow is at its minimum.

At **Ain Fijeh** (just under 20 km from the Umawiyeen Square, off to the right below the main road) there are a few restaurants close to the railway station. The village owes its name (and its existence) to the spring which emerges here and once used to add to the waters of the Barada river, though it is now piped directly to Damascus to supply the city's drinking water.

The small village of **Souq Wadi Barada** (28 km) stands on the site of the ancient Hellenistic town of **Abila**, which grew into an important centre on the route between Baalbek and Damascus. According to legend, it was on the mountain of Nebi Habil to the west of here that Cain buried Abel after killing him; hence the town's name. The only remains of the Hellenistic town, however, are in the occasional recycled architectural fragments to be found built into some of the houses.

Less than 2 km beyond the village, a series of rectangular doorways can be seen cut into the rock face on the opposite side of the now much narrowed gorge, marking a set of **Roman tombs**. The neatly hewn vaults each contain several compartments to house sarcophagi. To the left of the tombs (facing them from the road) a section of **irrigation channel** is visible, also of Roman origin or perhaps earlier, cut into the side of the rock face. Beyond this and above the level of the irrigation channel, there is a short stretch of **Roman road**, well preserved as it passes through a cutting. This is the road that connected Baalbek and Damascus. There are two inscriptions in the side of the cutting, both in Latin, which record how the road was restored following a landslide by the Legate Julius Verus, during the joint reign of Marcus Aurelius and Lucius Verus (AD 161-180). Reaching the tombs, irrigation channel or Roman road is rather tricky, and only for the sure-footed.

It is possible to **cross the gorge** from a point just past the Roman tombs, by walking across the rubbish-strewn bank from which the stream appears to emerge (if this is indeed one of the sources of the Barada, it can only be said that it starts as it means to go on), and then traversing a short though rather precarious section of concrete aqueduct to reach a path leading up to the tombs. Another option is to continue some 500 m along the modern road, around the corner to a point where a track leads off to the right. From here, double back along a track leading towards a small electricity pylon on a shoulder of the hillside. Just around the corner from this is the section of Roman road where it passes through a cutting. A little further on, it is possible to descend to the irrigation channel and follow it through a very deep and narrow cutting, followed by a short stretch of tunnel (not for the claustrophobic), and then past a couple of tricky sections where the outside wall has fallen away, to arrive at the tombs.

Continuing along the main road, after just under 3 km you reach what is in effect a T-junction. Bear right here (left to reach the Damascus–Beirut motorway) and follow the road for a further 12 km to reach Zabadani. This last stretch is across a broad, fertile plain boasting rich orchards of apples, apricots, walnuts, plums and cherries.

Zabadani

This popular hill resort has an affluent and, in summer at least, lively feel to it with plenty of well stocked shops along the main high street and a good selection of restaurants and cafés to choose from. Up on the hillside above the main town is a rapidly growing area of holiday homes owned by richer Syrians. The main high street, which crosses the railway line just by the station, is the focus for the modern town, with most of the shops, restaurants and cafés. Downhill from the station is 'old' Zabadani, quieter and more picturesque with an interesting old mosque in the centre and, close by, a Catholic church.

Getting there and away Regular microbuses run from the Al-Samariyeh bus station in Damascus (one hour, S£40) via the modern Beirut motorway. In Zabadani, microbuses cruise through the village picking people up for the return journey. If you have your own car, you can travel the far more picturesque route via the 'old' Zabadani road through the green and well-wooded Barada gorge (see above).

Bloudan

The town of Bloudan is situated 7 km to the east of Zabadani, at the slightly higher altitude of 1400 m. It is a smaller and somewhat more exclusive version of Zabadani, consisting mostly of modern concrete construction that has largely swamped the original Greek Orthodox and Catholic village out of which it grew. The main square is actually in the lower part of the town, and from here you can continue up the mountainside, passing ever more exclusive and fancy residences and restaurants along the way. Fridays are the best day to visit (this is true of Zabadani also), when the town is at its liveliest with day-trippers from Damascus, as well as visitors from Lebanon and Gulf-State holidaymakers.

Getting there and away As with Zabadani, microbuses from Damascus leave from Al-Samariyeh station but the services are not as frequent (one hour, S£40). If you want to visit both towns in the same day, note that there's no direct transport between the two and you'll have to hire a taxi from Zabadani.

If driving from Zabadani, the road hairpins its way up the mountainside, offering great views out over the valley below, before arriving in the town's main square.

Quneitra and the Golan Heights

Just 60 km to the southeast of Damascus are the Golan Heights, an area of high plateau between Mount Hermon and the northeastern shores of the Sea of Galilee, effectively marking the southern limits of the Anti-Lebanon mountains. Known in antiquity as the 'Gaulanitis' and then later as 'Jaulan', historically this area forms part of the wider Hauran region. Today it has become emblazoned in most people's minds as a potent symbol of the Arab-Israeli conflict.

Quneitra is a monument to the wanton destruction carried out by Israeli troops when they were forced to withdraw. It's a sad and depressing reminder of the continuing struggles of this region and how far there is still to go before they can be resolved.

Ins and outs
Getting there and away All visitors to Quneitra must obtain a **permit** in advance from the Ministry of the Interior in Damascus. Permits are free and are generally issued within around half an hour. However, they are only valid for 48 hours and you will need to have your own transport to be issued one (see page 62).

To drive from Damascus, head out of the city on the Mezzeh road (from Umawiyeen Square head southwest, keeping the Sheraton hotel on your right). Keep going straight to pass under the Beirut motorway (Quneitra is prominantly signposted straight ahead) and keep to this road all the way. After a while the looming outline of Mount Hermon comes clearly into view off to the right, often still streaked with snow as late as June. At the first check-post you come to, around 30 km from Damascus by a right turn signposted for Beit Saber, your permit and passport details are recorded in a book. A little further on, there are the remains of a large fortress on the right as you enter the town of Sa'asaa. Beyond Sa'asaa the countryside gives way to the distinctive rocky black basalt terrain of the Hauran. At Khan Arnabeh (61 km from Damascus) your permit and passport details will be recorded once again and a guide is assigned to show you around. It is a further 9 km on to Quneitra itself.

Background
Originally part of Syria, the Golan Heights were lost to Israel during the 1967 war. In 1973 Egypt and Syria launched simultaneous attacks on the Israeli-occupied Sinai and Golan Heights. Despite initial gains by Egypt and Syria, they were both subsequently pushed back and it was only in the negotiations following a ceasefire that Syria was able to regain some 450 sq km lost in the fighting. A UN-supervised demilitarized zone was established to separate the two sides, with Syria now administering this area under continued UN supervision.

The town of Quneitra today stands at the very edge of this demilitarized zone, with Israeli-occupied territory immediately beyond the barbed wire fences on its western outskirts. When the Israelis withdrew in 1973, they completely, and senselessly, demolished the town, leaving only the smashed, empty shells of buildings in their wake, and the Syrians have responded by leaving almost everything exactly as they found it, as a propaganda showcase against Israel.

Sights

You will be accompanied around the town by an official guide who is a Syrian army officer and is there for your safety (there are minefields in the area) only. You should tip your guide at the end of the 'tour'.

This battered ghost town has a sad, eerie atmosphere. Here, frozen in time, is an illustration of one of the great unresolved disputes of the Arab-Israeli conflict, a tangible episode of the modern history of the Middle East preserved in twisted metal and concrete. The UN military posts, the copious barbed wire and the Golan Heights themselves off to the west, all stand testimony to the continuing intractability of the dispute.

At the **hospital** you can inspect the heavily ruined shell of the building, while from the roof you can get good views over the town and the Golan Heights. Other prominent ruins include those of a **church** and a **mosque**. The **Liberated Quneitra Museum** is one of the few buildings to have been brought back into use. Housed in what was originally an Ottoman khan (of some interest in itself), the museum brings together a small collection of prehistoric, Roman and Byzantine artefacts; pottery, coins, architectural fragments, etc.

Following the main street to the very western extremity of the town, barbed wire marks the start of a stretch of **no man's land**, beyond which is effectively Israel. From the viewpoint you can see the two mountains to the east beyond the wide strip of cultivated land, the one to the left, bristling with the paraphernalia of Israel's observation and early warning systems, is Abou Nader, while the one to the right is Araam.

Around Damascus listings

🍴 Eating

Maaloula p63

Al-Barakeh, on the road to Deir Mar Sarkis. This friendly little restaurant has a shaded courtyard and does the usual mix of mezze and grills.

La Grotta, entrance to Deir Mar Sarkis. A modern little café with that's good for a refreshment stop after visiting the church. They do great sandwiches and they've got a nice outside terrace to relax in.

Saidnaya p66

For snacks and sandwich places head to the main street just below the Convent of Our Lady of Saidnaya.

Al-Massaya, main street below convent. Small but clean and pleasant restaurant serving reasonable food.

⚙ Festivals and events

Maaloula p63

14 Sep Exhaltation of the Holy Cross, Maaloula's most important feast day, when fires are lit on top of the cliffs and there is dancing and fireworks. **Feast of St Takla (24 Sep)**.

7 Oct Feast of St Sergius.

Saidnaya p66

7-8 Sep Feast of Our Lady of Saidnaya, Vast numbers of pilgrims, both Christian and Muslim, flock here every year for this event from all over the Middle East. People start

arriving here a couple of days before, with the main celebrations taking place on the night of 7 Sep, and being repeated again on a smaller scale on the following night. Around this time practically every available inch of floor space within the Convent of Our Lady of Saidnaya is taken up with pilgrims sleeping, praying, eating picnics, etc. Rooms at the town's only hotel, meanwhile, double in price and are soon all full.

🚌 Transport

Maaloula p63

Microbuses leave from the main intersection down the hill from Deir Mar Takla. To **Damascus** (1 hr, S£40) they leave frequently but start to peter out by early evening. To **Saidnaya** services aren't quite as regular but if you start off early enough from Damascus to Maaloula you can still quite easily do both Maaloula and Saidnaya in 1 day. If you want to go to **Deir Mar Musa** from Maaloula, catch the microbus to Saidnaya and change there for Nabak.

Saidnaya p66

Fairly frequent microbuses run from the main road in Saidnaya back to the the Maaloula Garage in **Damascus**, departing when full (1 hr, S£40). Public transport between Saidnaya and **Maaloula** is less frequent. Your best bet is to wait down on the main road and hitch; any traffic heading in that direction is sure to give you a lift. You can also get microbuses to **Nabak** (for Deir Mar Musa) from here.

Contents

Footnotes

Arabic words and phrases

Learning just a few basic words and phrases of Arabic is not at all difficult and will make an enormous difference to your travelling experience. Being able to greet people and respond to greetings, point at something in the souqs, ask 'how much?' and understand the reply – such simple things are rewarding, enjoyable and of practical benefit. The greatest hurdle most people face is with pronunciation. Arabic employs sounds which simply do not occur in English, so your tongue and mouth have to learn to form new, unfamiliar sounds. With a little patience, though, you can soon pick up the correct pronunciation of most words (or at least good enough to make yourself understood). The following is just a very brief introduction and the Arabic transliterations are simplistic: the bottom line is that there is no substitute for listening to and practicing with a native speaker. Once you are in the Middle East you will have plenty of opportunities to do this. But before you go, language books and tapes can get you started.

Greetings and pleasantries

hello (informal 'hi')	*marhaba*	fine, good, well	*qwayees*
hello ('welcome')	*ahlan wa sahlan* (or just *ahlan*)	please	*min fadlak/fadlik* (m/f)
hello ('peace be upon you')	*asalaam alaikum*	thank you	*shukran*
		thank you very much	*shukran jazeelan*
hello (response)	*wa alaikum as-salaam*	you're welcome	*afwan*
		sorry	*aassif*
goodbye	*ma'a salaama*	no problem	*ma fesh mushkilay*
good morning	*subah al-khair*	Congratulations!	*mabrouk!*
good morning (response)	*subah an-noor*	Thank God!	*il hamdullilah!*
good evening	*musa al-khair*	What is your name?	*shoo ismak/ismik?* (m/f)
good evening (response)	*musa an-noor*		
good night	*tusba allah khair*	My name is...	*ismi...*
good night (response)	*wa inta min ahalu*	Where are you from?	*min wain inta/inti?* (m/f)
How are you?	*kif halak/halik?* or *kifak/kifik* (m/f)	I am a tourist	*ana siyaha*

Useful expressions

If God wills it	*inshallah*	expensive	*ghaali*
yes	*naam/aiwa*	cheap	*rakhees*
no	*laa*	enough, stop	*hallas*
Where is .....?	*wain...?*	let's go	*yallah*
How far?	*kam kilometre?*	good	*qwayees*
Is there/do you have...?	*fi....?*	bad	*mish qwayees/ wahish*
There is	*fi*		
There is not, there's none	*ma fi*	I understand	*ana afham*
How much?	*bikam/adesh?*	I don't understand	*mish afham*

Getting around

airport	*al matar*	straight ahead	*ala tuul*
bus	*al bas/autobas*	tourist office	*makhtab siyaha*
bus station	*mahattat al bas/*	map	*khareeta*
	garagat	city centre/old city	*medina*
taxi	*taxi*	hotel	*funduq*
service taxi	*servees*	restaurant	*mataam/restauran*
train station	*mahattat al atr*	museum	*matthaaf*
car	*sayara*	bank	*masraf/banque*
left	*shimal*	chemist	*agzakhana*
right	*yameen*		

Documents

passport office	*makhtab al jawazaat*	name	*ism*
passport	*jawas as safar*	date of birth	*tarikha al mulid*
visa	*sima*	place of birth	*makan al mulid*
permit	*tasrih*	nationality	*jensiya*

Glossary

A

ablaq alternating courses of contrasting stone, typical of Mameluke and Ottoman architecture (Arabic)

acanthus a conventionalized representation of a leaf, used especially to decorate Corinthian columns

acropolis fortified part of upper city, usually containing a political, administrative, or religious complex

adyton inner sanctuary of the *cella* of a temple

agora open meeting place or market

amphora Greek or Roman vessel with a narrow neck and two handles, tapering at the base, used for transporting wine or oil

architrave lowest division of an *entablature* or decorated moulding round arch or window

apodyterium changing rooms of a Roman baths complex

apse semi-circular niche; in a Byzantine *basilica* this is always at the eastern end and contains the altar

atrium courtyard of a Roman house or forecourt of a Byzantine church

B

bab gate (Arabic)

barbican an outer defence, usually in the form of a tower, at the entrance to a castle

barrel vault a vault in the shape of a half-cylinder

basilica a Roman building/Byzantine church of rectangular plan with a central *nave* flanked by two side aisles and usually with an *apse* at one end

bastion strongpoint or fortified tower in fortifcations

beit house (Arabic)

bimaristan hospital, medical school (Arabic)

bir well (Arabic)

birkat pool or reservoir

burj tower (Arabic)

C

caldarium hot room in Roman baths complex

capital crowning feature of a column or pier

caravanserai see *khan* (Arabic)

cardo maximus main street of a Roman city, usually running north-south and lined with colonnades

castrum fortified Roman camp

cavea semi-circular seating in auditorium of Roman theatre

cella the inner sanctuary of a temple

chancel raised area around altar in a church

clerestory upper row of windows providing light to the nave of a church

colonette small, slender *column*

colonnade row of *columns* carrying *entablature*, or arches

column upright member, circular in plan and usually slightly tapering

crenellations battlements

cruciform cross-shaped

cuneiform script consisting of wedge-shaped indentations, usually made into a clay tablet, first developed by the Sumerians

cupola dome

D

decumanus major east-west cross-street in Roman city, intersecting with the *cardo maximus*

deir monastery (Arabic)

donjon (or keep) main fortified tower and last refuge of a castle

diwan see *iwan*

E

entablature horizontal stone element in Greek/Roman architecture connecting a series of columns, usually decorated with a cornice, frieze and architrave

exedra a recess in a wall or line of columns, usually semi-circular and traditionally lined with benches

F

forum open meeting place or market

fosse ditch or trench outside fortifications

frieze central section of *entablature* in classical architecture, or more generally any carved relief

frigidarium cold room in Roman baths complex

G

glacis (or *talus*) smooth sloping surface forming defensive fortification wall

groin vault two intersecting *barrel vaults* forming ceiling over square chamber, also called a cross vault

H

hammam bath house (Arabic)

haremlek private/family quarters of an Ottoman house (Arabic)

hypogeum underground burial chamber

I

iconostasis screen decorated with icons separating the *nave* and *chancel* of a Byzantine or Orthodox rite church

iwan (or *diwan/liwan*) open reception area off courtyard with high arched opening (Arabic)

J

Jami' Masjid Friday congregational mosque (Arabic)

jebel (or *jabal*) hill, mountain (Arabic)

K

kalybe open-fronted shrine with niches for statuary

keep see *donjon*

khan hostel and warehouse for caravans and traders consisting of walled compound with accommodation, stables/ storage arranged around a central courtyard (Arabic)

kufic early angular form of Arabic script (named after Kufa in southern Iraq)

L

lintel horizontal beam above doorway supporting surmounting masonry

liwan see *iwan*

loculus (plural *loculi*) shelf-like niche in wall of burial chamber for sarcophogus/ corpse

M

madrassa Islamic religious school (Arabic)

Mar Saint (Arabic)

maristan see *bimaristan*

masjid mosque (Arabic)

medina old city (Arabic)

mihrab niche, usually semi-circular and vaulted with a semi-dome, indicating direction of prayer (towards Mecca) (Arabic)

minaret tower of mosque

minbar pulpit in mosque for preaching, to right of *mihrab*

muezzin man who recites the call to prayer (Arabic)

N

narthex entrance hall to *nave* of church

nave the central rectangular hall of basilica/ church, usually lined with colonnades to separate it from the side-aisles

necropolis ancient burial ground

noria waterwheel (Arabic)

nymphaeum Roman monumental structure surrounding a fountain (dedicated to nymphs), usually with niches for statue

O

odeon small theatre or concert hall

orchestra paved semi-circular area between stage and *cavea* of Roman theatre

P

pediment triangular, gabled end to a classical building

peristyle colonnaded corridor running around the edges of a courtyard

pier vertical roof support

pilaster engaged pier or column projecting slightly from wall

portico colonnaded porch over outer section of doorway

praetorium Roman governor's residence or barracks

propylaeum monumental entrance to a temple

Q

qadi Muslim judge (Arabic)

qalat castle, fortress (Arabic)

qibla marking direction of prayer, indicated in a mosque by the *mihrab* (Arabic)

qubba dome (Arabic)

R

revetment facing or retaining wall in fortification

ribat Muslim pigrim hostel or hospice

S

sacristy small room in a church for storing sacred vestments, vessels, etc

salemlek area of Ottoman house for receiving guests

sanjak subdivision of an Ottoman *vilayet*

scaenae frons decorated stone façade behind the stage area of Roman theatre

seraya (or *serai*) palace (Arabic)

soffit the underside of a lintel

souq market (Arabic)

stela (plural *stelae*) narrow upright slab of stone, usually inscribed

T

talus see *glacis*

tariq road

tell artificial mound

temenos sacred walled temple enclosure surrounding *cella*

tepidarium warm room of a Roman baths complex

tessera (plural *tesserae*) small square pieces of stone used to form mosaic

tetrapylon arrangement of columns (usually four groups of four) marking major street intersections (eg between *cardo maximus* and *decumanus*) in Roman city

transept transverse section between nave and apse of church, giving a cruciform (cross) shape instead of basic rectangular shape

triclinium dining room of Roman house

tympanum the space enclosed in a *pediment*, or between a lintel and the arch above

V

via sacra sacred way used by pilgrims to approach shrine, etc

vilayet Ottoman adminsistrative province

vomitorium (plural *vomitoria*) entrance/exit to the seating area, or *cavea*, of a Roman theatre

W

wadi valley or watercourse with seasonal stream (Arabic)

Arabic cuisine → For food and drink, see page 9.

Bread

Known in Arabic as *khubz* or *eish* (literally 'life'), bread is the mainstay of the Arabic diet. It is baked unleavened (without yeast) in flat round discs and accompanies just about every meal or snack. Often it serves as an eating implement, or is rolled up with a filling inside to make a 'sandwich' snack. When it is fresh it is delicious although, surprisingly for a region where so much of it is consumed, it has often been standing about for the best part of a day by the time it reaches your plate.

Mezze dishes

Perhaps the most attractive feature of Arabic cuisine is the *mezze*. When done properly, this consists of a spread of numerous small dips, salads and nibbles of fresh raw vegetables, olive, etc, which are served as an extended starter course and, if the company is not teetotal, usually washed down with plenty of beer or arak. To fully appreciate a proper *mezze* spread you really need to be in a group of several people or you'll never get around the array of dishes; it also works out very reasonably when divided amongst several people. For smaller numbers you can just ask for a selection. If you do not want a full meal, you can always do away with the main courses and just concentrate on the *mezze*. Many of the items listed below are also served individually as a side dish in snack places and simple restaurants, or indeed as snacks in themselves. A selection of the more popular *mezze* dishes is given here.

baba ganoush (*moutabbal*) chargrilled eggplant (aubergine), tahini, olive oil, lemon juice and garlic blended into a smooth paste and served as a dip
falafel small deep-fried balls of ground, spiced chickpeas. Very popular, both as part of a *mezze*, and as the basis of one of Syria most ubiquitous snacks (see below)
fattoush salad of toasted croutons, cucumbers, tomatoes, onion and mint
hummus purée of chickpeas, tahini, lemon and garlic, served as a dip with bread
kibbeh ground lamb and bulghur (cracked wheat) meatballs stuffed with olives and pine nuts and fried or baked

kibbeh nayeh raw kibbeh, eaten like steak tartare
loubieh (*fasulya*) cooked French beans with tomatoes onion and garlic, served hot as a stew or cold as a kind of salad
mouhammara mixture of ground nuts, olive oil, cumin and chillis, eaten with bread
rocca rocket salad
tabouleh finely chopped salad of burghul wheat, tomatoes, onions, mint and parsley
taratour thick mayonnaise of puréed pine nuts, garlic and lemon, used as a dip
warak enab (*warak dawali*) vine leaves stuffed with rice and vegetables

'Main' meat dishes

So-called 'main' courses are more limited and consist primarily of meat dishes (usually lamb or chicken). Note that many listed below are also often served as snacks.

bamia baby okra and lamb in a tomato stew
bukhari rice lamb and rice stir-fried with onion, lemon, carrot and tomato

farouj roast chicken. Everywhere you go throughout Syria you will find simple restaurants, snack places and shops with roasting ovens outside containing several spits of roasting chickens. The standard portion is a half chicken (*nuss farouj*), sometimes served with a small portion of garlic dip and a few pickled vegetables and chips

kebab in Syria, if you ask for 'kebab', you will most likely be offered *kofte kebab*, though strictly speaking *kebab* is just chunks of meat char-grilled on a skewer

kofte kebab minced meat and finely chopped onions, herbs and spices pressed onto a skewer and chargrilled. You often

order by weight

kouzi whole lamb baked over rice so that it soaks up the juice of the meat

mensaf a traditional Bedouin dish, consisting of lamb cooked with herbs in a yoghurt sauce and served on a bed of rice with pine nuts. You are most likely to come across this dish at Palmyra

saleek lamb and rice dish cooked in milk

shish taouk fillets of chicken breast chargrilled on a skewer. Extremely popular and on offer in practically every restaurant

Fish

The price of fish tends to be expensive, though from mid-October to mid-November supplies are more plentiful and prices fall correspondingly. It is most commonly either grilled or fried and served with lemon, salad and chips.

gambari prawns

hamour Red Sea fish of the grouper family

najil saddle-back grouper

samak nahri trout

sayyadiya delicately spiced fish (usually red mullet or bass) served with rice

shaour Red Sea fish of the emperor family

Sultan Ibrahim red mullet (literally 'King Abraham', ie the king of fishes)

Snacks

Traditional snack bars (and indeed many restaurants) serve a wide range of snacks. If you are on a tight budget, or are a vegetarian, many of these will become staples.

ejje omelette, usually with chopped onion and herbs

falafel the *falafel* sandwich must be the most ubiquitous snack throughout Syria; you will find snack bars serving this (and often only this) everywhere you go. Several *falafel* balls (see under *mezze* dishes) are crushed on an open piece of Arabic bread, garnished with salad and pickled vegetables (usually tomatoes, beetroot, onion and lettuce), topped by a yoghurt and *tahini* sauce and then rolled up into a 'sandwich'. They are very cheap and filling, though if you are on a tight budget and relying on them as a staple, they can get pretty monotonous. The freshness of the bread, as well as the filling, is what makes or breaks them

fatayer triangular pastry pockets filled with spinach, meat or cheese. These make great snacks and are usually sold from bakeries

fatteh an excellent, very filling snack consisting of *fuul* and *laban* mixed together with small pieces of bread and topped with pine nuts and melted butter. Also sometimes served with fried minced meat mixed in

fuul slow-cooked mash of fava beans and red lentils, dressed with lemon, olive oil and cumin, and sometimes a little yoghurt and *tahini* sauce. An excellent, filling and nutritious snack, traditionally a breakfast dish, though available any time of day

kushary staple of pasta, rice and lentils mixed with onions, chilli and tomato paste. More common in Egypt, but found also in Syria

mannoushi thin, crusty 'pizzas' topped with a thin layer of meat (*Lahmeh*), cheese (*Jebneh*) or *Zaatar*, a seasoning with thyme and *sumac*

'sandweech' both *falafels* and *shawarmas* are commonly referred to simply as 'sandweech'. In addition, there are numerous other fillings available in many snack bars

shawarma this is essentially a meat version of a *falafel* sandwich, and an equally ubiquitous snack bar favourite. Layers of lamb or chicken roasted on a vertical spit are sliced off into small flat breads and rolled up with salad, pickled vegetables and a garlic sauce into a sandwich which is then steeped in extra fat as a special favour. Again they are cheap and filling, and if you are on a tight budget and not a vegetarian you will no doubt be eating plenty of them

Dairy products

Some of these make an appearance in other dishes listed here, or else are popular as drinks in their own right.

ayran salty yoghurt drink, good refreshing rehydration material

halab milk

jebneh (*Jibni*) fairly hard and stringy white cheese

laban slightly sour yoghurt drink, also widely used in cooking as a milk substitute

labneh thick creamy cheese, often spiced and used as a dip, for example *Labneh Maa Toum*, with garlic and olive oil

Sweets

The range of sweets, pastries, biscuits and puddings on offer is enormous, but they all share one thing in common: copious amounts of sugar in one form or another. Most are served at restaurants, but to see the full range of what's on offer you should go to a patisserie, where you will be confronted by a bewildering selection. Many patisseries also have an area where you can sit and eat, and some also serve tea, coffee and soft drinks.

asabeeh rolled filo pastry filled with pistachios, pine nuts and cashews and honey

atait small pancakes stuffed with nuts or cheese and doused with syrup

baklawa layered pastry filled with nuts and steeped in honey and lemon syrup. Probably the most common and best known Arabic sweet

barazak crisp, light biscuits sprinkled with sesame seeds

basboosa semolina tart soaked in syrup

booza ice cream

borma crushed pine nuts or pistachios wrapped in shredded pastry and sliced into segments

halawat al-jebneh soft thick pastry stuffed with *labneh* cheese and steeped in syrup and ice cream

halwa a sweet made from sesame paste, usually studded with fruit and nuts and made in a slab

kamar ed-dine apricot nectar, often served as a break of fast during Ramadan

kunafi pastry stuffed with sweet white cheese, nuts and syrup

ma'amul biscuits stuffed with date, pistachio or walnut paste

muhalabiyyeh fine, smooth textured semolina and milk pudding, sometimes with pistachios, pine nuts and almonds, served cold

sanioura dry, crumbly macaroon-like biscuit

um ali literally 'Ali's mother', a pastry pudding with raisin and coconut, steeped in milk

um ali literally 'Ali's mother', a pastry pudding with raisin and coconut, steeped in milk

Drinks

ahwa (or *Kahweh*) coffee The Arab attitude to coffee is basically the stronger the better. The coffee is boiled up in tiny pots and served very strong in equally tiny cups, complete with a thick sludge of coffee grounds at the bottom. It is served without sugar (*sadah*), with medium sugar (*wassad*), or with lots of sugar (*helweh*). Cardamom is sometimes added to give a delicate aromatic flavour. Instant coffee is referred to everywhere as 'Nescafe' and is available on request in most places

arak Arabic equivalent of the Greek *oozo* or Turkish *raki*, a potent liqueur made from grapes (in fact the leftovers of wine pressing) and flavoured with aniseed. It is very popular and is usually drunk with ice and/or cold water which make the otherwise clear alcohol go a cloudy white

shay tea Generally drunk strong and black, and with copious amounts of sugar. Mint tea and green tea are also available, though not so popular.

narghile (or *shisha*) not exactly an item of 'cuisine', the narghile nevertheless goes hand in hand with eating and drinking. It consists of a large water-pipe, known also as a *shish*, through which tobacco, often flavoured with apple or strawberry, is smoked. *Narghiles* are enjoyed at great length in cafés throughout Syria alongside tea and coffee and endless games of cards and backgammon, or else after a meal

Index

Titles available in the Footprint *Focus* range

Latin America	UK RRP	US RRP
Bahia & Salvador	£7.99	$11.95
Buenos Aires & Pampas	£7.99	$11.95
Costa Rica	£8.99	$12.95
Cuzco, La Paz & Lake Titicaca	£8.99	$12.95
El Salvador	£5.99	$8.95
Guadalajara & Pacific Coast	£6.99	$9.95
Guatemala	£8.99	$12.95
Guyana, Guyane & Suriname	£5.99	$8.95
Havana	£6.99	$9.95
Honduras	£7.99	$11.95
Nicaragua	£7.99	$11.95
Paraguay	£5.99	$8.95
Quito & Galápagos Islands	£7.99	$11.95
Recife & Northeast Brazil	£7.99	$11.95
Rio de Janeiro	£8.99	$12.95
São Paulo	£5.99	$8.95
Uruguay	£6.99	$9.95
Venezuela	£8.99	$12.95
Yucatán Peninsula	£6.99	$9.95

Asia	UK RRP	US RRP
Angkor Wat	£5.99	$8.95
Bali & Lombok	£8.99	$12.95
Chennai & Tamil Nadu	£8.99	$12.95
Chiang Mai & Northern Thailand	£7.99	$11.95
Goa	£6.99	$9.95
Hanoi & Northern Vietnam	£8.99	$12.95
Ho Chi Minh City & Mekong Delta	£7.99	$11.95
Java	£7.99	$11.95
Kerala	£7.99	$11.95
Kolkata & West Bengal	£5.99	$8.95
Mumbai & Gujarat	£8.99	$12.95

Africa	UK RRP	US RRP
Beirut	£6.99	$9.95
Damascus	£5.99	$8.95
Durban & KwaZulu Natal	£8.99	$12.95
Fès & Northern Morocco	£8.99	$12.95
Jerusalem	£8.99	$12.95
Johannesburg & Kruger National Park	£7.99	$11.95
Kenya's beaches	£8.99	$12.95
Kilimanjaro & Northern Tanzania	£8.99	$12.95
Zanzibar & Pemba	£7.99	$11.95

Europe	UK RRP	US RRP
Bilbao & Basque Region	£6.99	$9.95
Granada & Sierra Nevada	£6.99	$9.95
Málaga	£5.99	$8.95
Orkney & Shetland Islands	£5.99	$8.95
Skye & Outer Hebrides	£6.99	$9.95

North America	UK RRP	US RRP
Vancouver & Rockies	£8.99	$12.95

Australasia	UK RRP	US RRP
Brisbane & Queensland	£8.99	$12.95
Perth	£7.99	$11.95

For the latest books, e-books and smart phone app releases, and a wealth of travel information, visit us at: www.footprinttravelguides.com.

footprinttravelguides.com

Join us on facebook for the latest travel news, product releases, offers and amazing competitions: www.facebook. com/footprintbooks.com.